KURT VONNEGUT

In the same series:

(*continued on page 125*)

MODERN LITERATURE MONOGRAPHS
GENERAL EDITOR: Lina Mainiero

KURT VONNEGUT

James Lundquist

FREDERICK UNGAR PUBLISHING CO.
NEW YORK

Copyright © 1977 by Frederick Ungar Publishing Co., Inc.
Printed in the United States of America
Designed by Anita Duncan

Library of Congress Cataloging in Publication Data

Lundquist, James.
  Kurt Vonnegut.

  (Modern literature monographs)
  Bibliography: p.
  Includes index.
  1. Vonnegut, Kurt—Criticism and interpretation.
PS3572.05Z76   813'.5'4   76–15654
ISBN 0–8044–2564–7

Second Printing, 1977

Contents

Chronology

1922   Kurt Vonnegut is born 11 November 1922 in
            Indianapolis, Indiana, to Kurt and Edith Leiber
            Vonnegut.

1940   Graduates from Shortridge (Indianapolis) High
            School, where he wrote for the *Daily Echo*, the
            student newspaper.

1940–41   Attends Cornell University, where he planned to
            major in chemistry. Works on Cornell *Daily Sun*

1942   Enters U.S. Army.

1944   Mother dies, 14 May. Vonnegut captured by Ger-
            mans during Battle of the Bulge in December.

1945   Lives through firebombing of Dresden, 13 Febru-
            ary. Released in April.

1945–47   Marries Jane Marie Cox. Attends University of
            Chicago. Works as reporter for Chicago City News
            Bureau. M.A. thesis in anthropology, "Fluctuations
            Between Good and Evil in Simple Tales," not ac-
            cepted.

1947   Goes to work for General Electric Corporation,
            Schenectady, New York, as research laboratory
            publicist.

1950   Leaves General Electric to devote full time to
            writing. Story, "Report on the Barnhouse Effect,"
            published in *Collier's*, 11 February.

1952   First novel, *Player Piano*, published by Scribners.

1953   *Player Piano* published by Doubleday Science Fic-
            tion Book Club.

1957   Father dies, 1 October.

1959   *Sirens of Titan* published as paperback original by Dell.

1961   *Canary in a Cat House*, collection of short stories, published as paperback original by Gold Medal Books (Fawcett).

1962   *Mother Night* published as paperback original by Gold Medal Books.

1963   *Cat's Cradle* published by Holt, Rinehart and Winston.

1965   *God Bless You, Mr. Rosewater* published by Holt, Rinehart and Winston. Vonnegut in residence at the University of Iowa Writer's Workshop.

1966–67   *Player Piano* republished as hardback by Holt, Rinehart and Winston, *Mother Night* by Harper and Row.

1967–68   In Dresden on Guggenheim Fellowship.

1968   *Welcome to the Monkey House*, collection of short stories, published by Delacorte.

1969   *Slaughterhouse-Five* published by Delacorte.

1970   Teaches writing at Harvard University.

1970–71   *Happy Birthday, Wanda June*, play, produced in New York City, adapted for film, and is published by Delacorte.

1971   Awarded M.A. degree from the University of Chicago (*Cat's Cradle* seen as a significant work in anthropology).

1972   *Between Time and Timbuktu*, teleplay based on excerpts from Vonnegut's short stories and novels, is produced as NET special and published by Delacorte. Movie version of *Slaughterhouse-Five* released.

1973   *Breakfast of Champions* published by Delacorte and becomes the main selection of three book clubs (The Literary Guild, Book Find, and Saturday Review). Selected sections from the early chapters are printed in *Ramparts*, February. Vonnegut replaces Anthony Burgess as Distinguished Professor of English Prose at City University of New York.

1974   *Wampeters, Foma, & Granfalloons,* an assortment of reviews, essays, and speeches published by Delacorte.

1976   *Slapstick* is published.

1

Report on
the Vonnegut Effect

One thing is apparent from the start in reading Vonnegut: he is an enthusiast of sentimental detachment, a Pinball Wizard of cosmic cool who, through the charm of his style and the subtle challenge of his ideas, encourages us to adopt his interplanetary midwestern viewpoint and to believe once again in such radically updated values as love, compassion, humility, and conscience. He is a dervish of paradox as he suggests in his extended fables that we must learn to maintain happy illusions over villainous ones, that the best truth is a comforting lie, and that if there is any purpose to human history, it is best understood as a joke—at our expense.

There is a mystical, perhaps unnerving appeal in the way Vonnegut artistically maintains the clement aloofness that strangely accounts for much of his contemporaneity; but behind it all, behind the fantasy and the anti-establishmentarianism, is a deceptive fondness for the uncomplicated that enchants some readers, repels others, and seems downright anti-intellectual or, worse, silly to his least sympathetic critics. Which of the three reactions is most valid is a matter of taste or tastelessness (depending on how you look at it); but how Vonnegut, a distinctly bourgeois writer who has more in common with Sinclair Lewis than with Hermann Hesse, came to achieve his present reputation and whether his artistry will sustain it is another matter.

Kurt Vonnegut was born on the 11th of November 1922 in Indianapolis, Indiana. The date and the place of birth are important—the date because it guaranteed Vonnegut the two experiences that most seem to have shaped his thought and development, the great depression and World War II; and the place because it gave him the midwestern attitudes that so color the often contradictory sentiments that run through the novels that have established him as a genius of popular culture and a self-acknowledged poisoner of the minds of youth.

The impact of World War II on Vonnegut is well known and will receive considerable discussion later. The facts are that he was taken prisoner by the Germans during the Battle of the Bulge in 1944 and survived the fire-bombing of Dresden in the cellar of a slaughterhouse. This experience is central to two of his novels, *God Bless You, Mr. Rosewater* and *Slaughterhouse-Five*, is important to *Mother Night*, and lends authenticity to Vonnegut's pacifism. But despite the emphasis Vonnegut places on the Dresden holocaust and what it has come to symbolize in his novels, he places nearly equal stress on what he learned growing up during the 1930s.

The depression early impressed Vonnegut with the enormous amount of suffering in the world—suffering caused mainly by the loss of self-respect forced upon people by economic conditions beyond their control. Vonnegut has said that the depression "has more to do with the American character than any war. People felt useless for so long. The machines fired everybody. . . . I saw and listened to thousands of people who couldn't follow their trades anymore, who couldn't feed their families. A hell of a lot of them didn't want to go on much longer. They wanted to die because they were so embarrassed."[1] Along with this insight into American character, Vonnegut learned a compensating idealism during his adolescence at School 43 in Indianapolis. "America was an idealistic, pacifistic nation at the time," Vonnegut has said in recalling the 1930s. "I was taught in the sixth grade to be proud that we had a standing army of just over a hundred thousand men and that the generals had nothing to say about what was done in Washington. I was taught to be proud of that and to pity Europe for having more than a million men under arms and spending all their money on airplanes and tanks. I simply never un-learned junior civics. I still believe in it. I got a very good grade."[2]

Vonnegut's emphasis on the need for self-respect and his belief in the necessity of pacifism point to traits of character that are, one may argue, very much mid-western. Vonnegut's work can be read almost as if it is designed to illustrate attitudes that John T. Flanagan, a major apologist for the region, sees as particularly mid-western: "individualism, self-reliance, a practical materialism, skepticism of custom and tradition unless rooted in common sense, political intransigence, and isolationism explained and heretofore justified by the geographical barriers and almost antagonistic apathy of the Old World."[3]

Even Vonnegut's obsession with science-fiction techniques can be understood in terms of his regional background. "Vonnegut's fondness for vistors from other worlds is the drollest expression yet of the midwestern feeling that the Midwest *is* the Earth and that all other people are different," Alfred Kazin writes. "All that has changed since the West was the country of innocence is Vonnegut's feeling that innocence is dangerous."[4] Vonnegut shares this feeling with Mark Twain, Sherwood Anderson, Sinclair Lewis, and other midwestern writers; but given Vonnegut's sense of imminent apocalypse, the feeling is expressed with much more urgency and is more to the point than ever.

Vonnegut returns to the midwest again and again for characters and settings. The novelist Dan Wakefield (*Going All the Way*), who also hails from Vonnegut

country, points out that in each of Vonnegut's books
there is at least one character from Indianapolis and
compares this to Alfred Hitchcock's practice of making a
walk-on appearance in each of his movies.[4] Vonnegut can
even be seen as a literary embodiment of the midwest-
erner in the updated tradition of the vernacular storyteller, according to one commentator, "shuffling or
buttonholing, offering himself as someone very open, very
loose, very involved with the reader, who is presumed
always to be a 'like spirit.' "[5]

This is an appealing approach and it may be a good
reason for the success Vonnegut has had with a contemporary reading audience that uneasily accepts alienation
as a fact of life. Even though the stability, the security,
and the optimism associated with middle-class, midwestern attitudes are no longer to be found in Indianapolis or
anywhere else, Vonnegut remains something of a home-
sick writer. In all of his attacks on pornography, pollution, war, and whatever other evils he chooses to name,
there is an inescapable longing for an earlier, simpler
time, for the midwest of his boyhood or, to make what at
first seems to be an extravagant claim, to the Indianapolis
of Booth Tarkington.

Tarkington, like Vonnegut, had the "fractured vision"[6] that may well be characteristic of midwestern
writers. Now considerably neglected, Tarkington (1869–
1946) was an immensely popular novelist whose books
demonstrate considerable artistry, but always lack resolution. Tarkington was interested in realism and sought to
capture the condition of life as accurately as he could;
but his own temperament forced him to revaluate those
conditions in softer terms. *The Conquest of Canaan*
(1905), with its grim depiction of small-town brutality
and its nonetheless happy ending, is an example.

Vonnegut seems to be influenced by his own essentially sentimental temperament in much the same way,
although cultural changes have made the results consid-

erably different. At the same time he suggests (and
knows) that the world is absurd, Vonnegut emphasizes
the importance of humanitarian moral values, especially
the value of uncritical love and a sense of family, a sense
of belonging somewhere. At the same time he proclaims
the impossibility of belief, he asks us "to believe in the
most ridiculous superstition of all: that humanity is at the
center of the universe, the fulfiller or the frustrator of the
grandest dreams of God Almighty."[7]

This split in Vonnegut's outlook is understandable
enough. It grew out of the shattered optimism that was a
result not just of Dresden but of the sequence of events
that led to the destruction of the old emphasis on midwestern humanitarian values; it grew out of American
history since 1922, experienced from the vantage point of
Indianapolis. But there is more to it than that, because
there were many early influences on Vonnegut that
served to considerably reinforce the impact of his surroundings.

One, of course, was his family. "My ancestors, who
came to the United States a little before the Civil War,
were atheists," Vonnegut once said. "So I'm not rebelling
against organized religion. I never had any. I learned my
outrageous opinions about organized religion at my
mother's knee. My family has always had these. They
came here absolutely crazy about the United States Constitution and about the possibility of prosperity and the
brotherhood of man here. They were willing to work very
hard and they were atheists."[8] Vonnegut's father was a
well-known architect in Indianapolis, as was his grand-
father, who was the first licensed architect in Indiana. So
Vonnegut grew up in a family that emphasized freethink-
ing, rationalism, and the development of some sensitivity
to art.

But both of his parents, according to him, lived with
constant sadness, attributed by Vonnegut to their belief
that the world they loved had been destroyed by World

War I. "I'm grateful that I learned from them that organized religion is anti-Christian and that racial preju-
dices are stupid and cruel," Vonnegut said. "I'm grateful,
too, that they were good at making jokes. But I also
learned a bone-deep sadness from them."⁹

The jokes, the sadness, both eventually became
Vonnegut's trademark. But his parents were not able to
resolve their contradictory impulses, their own fractured
visions, so fortunately. Vonnegut's mother died of an
overdose of sleeping pills in 1944. As for his father, this
is what Vonnegut has said: "After I'm gone, I don't want
my children to have to say about me what I have to say
about my father: 'He made wonderful jokes, but he was
such an unhappy man.' "¹⁰

As important as Vonnegut's parents were to his
development as a writer, a more direct influence was the
Shortridge High School *Echo*, one of the few high-school
papers to be published daily. Instead of having to write
for just one person—usually a teacher—as most beginning writers must do, Vonnegut had a large audience
from the start. And if he did a bad job, he heard about it
from a lot of people within twenty-four hours. "It just
turned out," Vonnegut said in looking back on his experience with the *Echo*, "that I could write better than a
lot of other people. Each person has something he can do
easily and can't imagine why everybody else has so much
trouble doing it. In my case it was writing."¹¹

From Shortridge High School, Vonnegut, in a move
common to many other midwestern writers, went east to
college—Cornell University, where he studied biochemis-
try. Before his freshman year was over, however, he was
writing for the Cornell *Daily Sun*, taking over "Innocents
Abroad," a column in which he reprinted jokes lifted
from other publications.¹² Vonnegut thus began his
career at Cornell in the genre of "college humor," a type
of writing that had already produced James Thurber,
Robert Benchley, Dorothy Parker, and S. J. Perelman.

But the genre presented what was to prove a lasting problem for Vonnegut—how to be funny at a time when the world seems to be going to hell. "With Adolf Hitler, labor riots, and the ongoing amusement of current events, the funny side of things is not so apparent," he wrote in his first piece.

Vonnegut was soon doing an original column, "Well All Right," and he moved on to write a series of pacifistic articles. In one, he made fun of the naïve enthusiasm of newly-recruited soldiers ("Bayonet Drill at the Rate of Seven in 20 Seconds, or, Oh for a Couple of Nazis"). He also wrote pieces about the slanting of events in newspaper stories covering the invasion of Crete, and the phoniness in the way a magazine article was put together on the Cornell ROTC program ("We Impress *Life* Magazine with Our Efficient Role in National Defense"). One column was a passionate defense of the isolationism of Charles A. Lindbergh ("We Chase a Lone Eagle and End Up on the Wrong Side of the Fence"). His Lindbergh article was published with an appended editor's note indicating that the writer's opinions did not reflect the views of the *Sun*. Years later, Vonnegut remembered his "Well All Right" columns as impudent but congenial editorializing, adding that he has always had to have an ax to grind.[13]

His humorous ax-grinding temporarily came to an end when World War II arrived and he entered the U. S. Army in 1942. After his release from the service, he returned to the United States and married Jane Marie Cox (they had met in kindergarten in Indianapolis). He began work on an M. A. in anthropology at the University of Chicago, but his thesis, "Fluctuations Between Good and Evil in Simple Tales," was not accepted. While in graduate school, he worked as a reporter for the Chicago City News Bureau. In 1947 he went to work for the General Electric Corporation in Schenectady, New York, as a research-laboratory publicist. In addition to gather-

ing information for and working on his first novel, *Player
Piano* (1952), Vonnegut began to sell stories to *Collier's*
magazine and the *Saturday Evening Post*, gaining enough
confidence to leave General Electric in 1950 and devote
full time to writing.

Vonnegut then entered what, to many, has seemed
the least successful part of his career. His second novel,
Sirens of Titan, was not published until 1959. When
Esquire, in the middle 1950s, printed a list claiming to
include every living American writer of even the slightest
merit, Vonnegut's name was not on it. And it would be
1966 before a scholarly article about his work would be
published. But throughout the 1950s Vonnegut managed
to support himself and his family (three children—Mark,
Edith, and Nanette—and three adopted nephews, James,
Steven, and Kurt Adams, the children of his deceased
sister) reasonably well through writing short stories and
non-fiction for the popular magazines.

This writing, which has been disparaged by many
critics, is hack work only in a sense. Vonnegut's short
stories are no worse than many of the slick stories of the
same type written by Fitzgerald; and in some ways, perhaps as expressions of sentiment genuinely felt by the
writer, they are better. Not all of the stories are worth
reading, or even worth mentioning, but some show Vonnegut's imagination and humor at their near best, and most
of them demonstrate that from the start Vonnegut knew
how to tell a good story. An example is "Report on the
Barnhouse Effect" (published in *Collier's*, 11 Feb.
1950), in which a professor learns to utilize his psychic
powers to become "the most powerful weapon on earth"
after he throws ten consecutive sevens in a crap game.
But, as a reviewer of *Welcome to the Monkey House* (a
collection of short stories and non-fiction published in
1968) indicates, in a comment that could just as well
apply to the majority of Vonnegut's stories, "far too
many of the selections in this pseudobook are mere

contrivances or tearjerkers."[14] Another reviewer frankly states an opinion that is shared by Vonnegut himself: "They were stories written to sell . . . and they carry along a burdensome weight of disguise."[15]

But while Vonnegut was plugging away at his short-story writing, his reputation was quietly growing underground. College students, haunters of the paperbook bookracks at bus stations and airports, and other mysterious people were reading and talking about *Player Piano, The Sirens of Titan, Mother Night,* and *Cat's Cradle.* Honors eventually followed. In 1965 Vonnegut was in residence at the University of Iowa Writer's Workshop. His novels were reissued in paperback in 1966. And in 1967 and 1968 he returned to Dresden on a Guggenheim Fellowship.

By the time *Cat's Cradle* appeared in 1963, some of the critical acceptance of Vonnegut's work had become downright enthusiastic. Terry Southern, in an appreciation he wrote for the *New York Times Book Review,* claimed of *Cat's Cradle* that, "Like the best of contemporary satire, it is a work of a far more engaging and meaningful order than the melodramatic tripe which most critics seem to consider 'serious.' "[16] Unlike other writers with whom he has long been compared, John Barth and Thomas Pynchon to name two, Vonnegut's "engaging and meaningful order" places him within the range, stylistically at least, of a popular audience; and it is Vonnegut's appeal to that audience that Leslie Fiedler sees as one of the most significant aspects of Vonnegut's achievement.

Fiedler believes that the so-called death of the novel, which has concerned critics for years, is better understood as the death of the "art" novel—the type of novel in the Proust-Mann-Joyce tradition that is read by an elite audience. Emerging in place of the art novel are the popular forms—westerns, science fiction, and pornography—to which some current writers, such as Barth

and William Burroughs, have turned. Vonnegut's advantage in all of this is that he began as a pop writer in the
slick magazines. "Vonnegut *does* belong to what we
know again to be the mainstream of fiction," Fiedler
writes; "it is not the mainstream of High Art, however,
but of myth and entertainment: a stream which was
forced to flow underground over the past several decades,
but has now surfaced once more."[17]

Vonnegut is thus a transitional figure in a time when
the anti-egalitarian values of such earlier figures as T. S.
Eliot, who believed that culture is the property of the tiny
remnant that can appreciate highly abstruse and allusive
symbolic forms of art, are being left behind. Pop, which
has been seen as a vice of the populace, is now regarded
as a fantastic and fantastically valuable storehouse of
dreams, longings, and ancient myths retooled. What
Vonnegut as a pop novelist does, in part, is what he
himself attributes to Hunter S. Thompson: "He makes
exciting, moving collages of carefully selected junk. They
must be experienced. They can't be paraphrased."[18]

Much of Vonnegut's writing employs the formula of
science fiction, makes use of stock characters (often
bizarrely represented, however), replays old plots
(Vonnegut's admitted rip-off of *Brave New World* in
Player Piano is but one example), states universal
themes, and is written in a style that depends heavily on
folk sayings and street language. In just about every con-
ceivable way Vonnegut's novels are what only can be
termed "naïve" literature because he makes so much use
of expected associations and conventions for the purpose
of rapid communication with its readers. And what sets
other writers apart from popular audiences is the very
thing that Vonnegut seems to lack—sophistication. His
manner suggests to his readers that he is not looking
down on them, that he may even be right there, where
they are and where it's at.

Getting onto that level is by no means simple, however much it may seem so. "The particular power of Vonnegut's work—especially in the four books which develop his distinctive voice, all published in the 1960s—is in the deceptively simple way he deals with the extraordinary nature of contemporary fact," Raymond M. Olderman writes in his study of the recent American novel. "Vonnegut is a master of getting inside a cliché and tilting it enough off center to reveal both the horror and the misery that lies beneath the surface of the most placidly dull and ordinary human response."[19] Vonnegut's revelations are often accomplished through the use of fables, another of the naïve forms he likes to work in. His stories always have morals, and they work to expose sins and folly.

Vonnegut uses another, perhaps more complex, association or convention—the structural discontinuity that appeals to the imagination of an audience accustomed to the montage of television. This is part of Vonnegut's fragmented idiom, which in itself suggests contemporary experience. The way Vonnegut times the talk of his characters, along with his short chapters, his sharp images, and his quick scenes—all of this makes reading his fiction a formal approximation of the experience of watching television.[20]

But Vonnegut's popularity should not be interpreted only as a consequence of the modish appeal of his fiction or because his books make use of so many of the devices employed by the electronic media. Vonnegut's willingness to speak directly to his audience must have something to do with it. And what does he say to this audience? "I do moralize," he admits. "I tell them not to take more than they need, not to be greedy. I tell them not to kill, even in self-defense. I tell them not to pollute water or the atmosphere. I tell them not to raid the public treasury."[21] He further advises us not to work for any people who do these things, to avoid getting involved in war crimes, and to be kind.

"I've often thought there ought to be a manual to hand to little kids, telling them what kind of planet they're on, why they don't fall off it, how much time they've probably got here, how to avoid poison ivy, and so on," Vonnegut has said. "I tried to write one once. It was called *Welcome to Earth*. But I got stuck on explaining why we don't fall off the planet."[22] In a sense, all of Vonnegut's novels are *Welcome* books, full of attitudes and instructions on handling those attitudes that are useful if one is to avoid falling off the planet, or if one wishes to keep the planet here, wherever it is.

It is a mistake, however, to conceive of Vonnegut's significance entirely in terms of his popular success. Not only does he deal with concerns that are important to all of us, but he develops many ideas in startlingly refreshing ways. One surprising consideration is that Vonnegut is a thoroughly middle-class writer who is, in some of his work at least, an apologist for the very kind of life he seems to be attacking. Vonnegut writes from a vantage point that is consistently middle class, and in his novels there is the suggestion, repeated many times, that the most unhappy people are those who do not have the blessings of middle-class life—a point that Vonnegut often expresses with considerable sentimentality.

Vonnegut picked up his sentimentality early. When he was a boy, Vonnegut recalls, a black cook named Ida Young would read to him "from an anthology of sentimental poetry about love which would not die, about faithful dogs and humble cottages where happiness was, about people growing old, about visits to cemeteries, about babies who died. I remember the name of the book, and wish I had a copy, since it has so much to do with what I am."[23] The name of the book, which could just as well be used as the title of a collection of Vonnegut's short stories, was *More Heart Throbs*. From there, Vonnegut says it was an easy leap to *Spoon River Anthology* and *Main Street*. "There is an almost intolerable sentimentality beneath everything I write," he comments.[24] This sentimentality is fueled by a distinctly (and perhaps uniquely) middle-class variety of pity—feeling sorry for those who do not have it so good. This emotional response is central to Vonnegut's remedy for things. "Pity is like rust to a cruel social machine" is his idea.[25]

Vonnegut's pity can be seen at work in his account of visiting Biafra in January 1970 while it was under siege by Nigeria. There is painfully honest horror in Vonnegut's account, and his typical use of understatement makes it all the more so. He flew in on a DC-6 chartered by a Roman Catholic relief organization and had intended to write only about the greatness of Biafra, which he thought of as a nation of poets and intellectuals. But at the end he admits, "I have mourned the children copiously. I have told of a woman who was drenched in gasoline."[26] Vonnegut often comes across like his own Eliot Rosewater, a man filled with so much pity for humanity that it becomes, at times, unbearable.

Vonnegut's sentimentality is, of course, behind most of his social pronouncements and his remedy for the American experience, an experience he interprets as generally an unhappy one. One reason he sees for the unhappiness is that Americans suffer from living without a culture. In his view, American society is a lonesome one. He senses a longing for community, a longing that is frustrated by the shifting from house to house and from town to town that the economic system requires of so many Americans. Vonnegut not only believes that people should spend their lives in one place, he would restore the old emphasis on family relationships by having the government create an artificial extended family. Computers would assign, say, 20,000 people in the United States a middle name like Daffodil; and no matter where someone went, there would be a member of his "family" he could call up or see (an idea that receives extended treatment in Vonnegut's most recent novel, *Slapstick*). Vonnegut

would also prefer that people live in "primitive" com-
munities, folk societies, which he seems to think of in
terms of small towns or of neighborhoods within cities
(again the middle-class, midwestern vision of tree-shaded
streets and old, comfortable homes).

Consideration of such economic and social pronouncements might have no place in a study of Vonnegut's achievement as a writer if it were not for his often
stated opinion (which he wryly says is in agreement with
that of Stalin, Hitler, and Mussolini) that a writer should
serve society and that his own motives, at least, are political. "Writers are a means of introducing new ideas
into society," Vonnegut emphasizes, "and also a means
of responding symbolically to life."[27] His notion of what
a writer should do is in conflict, however, with his assumption (perhaps another middle-class suspicion) that
writers of fiction are simply not important and most certainly are not listened to by the government.

Despite the reputation he gained as an opponent of
the war in Vietnam, he thinks that all the opposition in
print to what was going on in southeast Asia had the
explosive power of a banana-cream pie. The only positive
result he can hope for is that he and other writers succeeded in "poisoning" the minds of young readers so they
will be of no use in unjust wars. "Our purpose is to make
mankind aware of itself, in all its complexity, and to
dream its dreams," he said in a 1973 address to the
P.E.N. Conference in Stockholm. "We have no choice in
the matter. Our influence is slow and subtle, and it is felt
mainly by the young. They are hungry for myths which
resonate with mysteries of their own times."[28]

The purpose of writing and of all the arts is to provide those myths or "frauds," as Vonnegut terms them,
which make man seem wonderful and important even if
we all know that in the long run he is not. "The arts put
man at the center of the universe, whether he belongs
there or not," he told the graduating class of Bennington

College in 1970. "Military science is probably right about the contemptibility of man in the vastness of the universe. Still—I deny that contemptibility, and I beg you to deny it, through the creation and appreciation of art."[29] So, even though each of Vonnegut's novels shows that man in general is contemptible, Vonnegut always has a hero who denies that contemptibility through his ability to come up with or live through a myth that is usually redemptive, somehow.

There is, however, another way Vonnegut views the usefulness of the arts. In his address to the American Physical Society in 1969, he said that in teaching writing, he has come up with what he calls the "canary-in-the-coal-mine theory of the arts." His explanation is "that artists are useful to society because they are so sensitive. . . . They keel over like canaries in coal mines filled with poison gas, long before more robust types realize that any danger is there."[30] His application of this theory is evident in all of his novels, each of which is a cry of danger, from *Player Piano* with its warning about computerization, to *Breakfast of Champions* with its warning about the consequences of failing to understand the chemical causes of schizophrenia.

This had led to some difficulty in understanding and accepting Vonnegut's often rather peculiar sort of novel. "We should read Vonnegut with some different criteria," one of Vonnegut's critics writes. "If we grant that he has designs on us and that he sometimes sacrifices fictive device for absolute clarity, often sounding more like a social scientist than a novelist, then we can forget his occasional failure to justify the literary tradition he half evokes, and judge him on the genuine quality of a passionately honest heart and mind working over the bewildering facts of contemporary existence."[31]

Vonnegut goes at those facts; and a close study of his work reveals that, for all his seeming simplicity, for all his public acceptance, he is deeply interested in epistemological questions of an impressive variety—the unreality of time, the problem of free will, the nature of a pluralistic universe, and man's ability to live with his own illusions. How he poses these questions and the extent to which he answers them can only come out of a direct consideration of his novels, and it is to this we turn next, examining first his humorous bitterness and then the form through which it is expressed.

2

Cosmic Irony

One of the stranger details Vonnegut gives us concerning the boyhood of Billy Pilgrim in *Slaughterhouse-Five* is that even though Billy was not a Catholic, there was a gruesome crucifix hanging on his bedroom wall. Vonnegut explains that Billy's mother, who was a substitute organist for several churches but a member of none, developed a powerful longing for a crucifix. So when she found one she liked in a Santa Fe knick-knack store while on a vacation trip out West, she bought it. "Like so many Americans," Vonnegut writes, "she was trying to construct a life that made sense from things she found in gift shops."

Vonnegut is a comic writer. His aside about Billy Pilgrim's mother and the Santa Fe crucifix is typical of his humor, which derives, as often as not, from the pathetically laughable attempts of human beings to either discover or impose order on the pluralistic universe in which they live. Mrs. Pilgrim has the same impulse so many of Vonnegut's characters have: she wants life to make sense. Vonnegut knows that it simply does not; and his readers soon learn that the answer is not to be found in Santa Fe. So Mrs. Pilgrim is a comic figure, and the allusion to the gift shop, with its pop-culture implications, adds to the "fun," such as it is. The term for this type of humor, and the term that works best overall in discussing Vonnegut's most distinctive feature, his comic vision, is cosmic irony—the laughable prospect of man's attempts to give order to the disorder of the universe through philosophies, theologies, or even scientific systems. In one way or another, each of Vonnegut's novels is an extended cosmically ironic joke.

Another term, black humor, has often been used in discussing Vonnegut's comedy and must also be taken into account in any extended consideration of his work even though black humor has never lent itself to the kind of definition that its suggestion of genre would, on face value, indicate. This is because black humor has its origin in a state of mind as much as anything—the state of mind that prevailed throughout most of the 1960s and received its impetus from televised body counts, assassinations, campus riots, and the drug culture.[1] But the roots go back to the absurdities of the cold war, the disappointments of Korea, the rise of Joe McCarthy, the Kefauver crime hearings, Nixon's Checkers speech, the race riots in Little Rock, and even the hula-hoop craze. The question invited by all of this was how to react. One response was laughter of a sort that initially seemed either peculiar or disgusting.

The first use of black humor as a critical description was in an article by Conrad Knickerbocker, "Humor with a Mortal Sting," that appeared in *The New York Times Book Review* (27 September 1964). Main credit for making the term widely known is given, however, to Bruce Jay Friedman, who edited a paperback anthology, *Black Humor*, which was published in 1965. In addition to Friedman himself, the anthology included twelve other writers: Terry Southern, J. P. Donleavy, Edward Albee, Louis-Ferdinand Céline, Joseph Heller, Thomas Pynchon, John Barth, John Rechy, Charles Simmons, James Purdy, Vladimir Nabokov, and Knickerbocker. Oddly enough, Vonnegut, whose name is one of those now most often associated with black humor, was not represented in the original thirteen. This in itself suggests some prob-

lems with both Friedman's selection and his use of the
term. The critic Robert Scholes, who elsewhere argues
for the validity of the concept of black humor, admits
that Friedman's employment of the term amounts to little
more than making it into a sales-promotion label.[2] And a
quick look at Friedman's anthology suggests that black
humor must incorporate the theatre of the absurd, exis-
tentialism, Irish whimsey, and that memorable phenomenon of the 1950s, the sick joke. As one commentator has
said, black humor seems to cover "everything from a
kind of generalized irreverence as in the macabre-joke
movies of Terry Southern and George Axelrod, to a sense
of doom so intense that the only possible reaction is hor-
rified laughter."[3]

But there are some stylistic features that Vonnegut
and these writers share. They like to take tragic material
and give it grotesquely comic treatment—the way
Vonnegut depicts the end of the world in *Cat's Cradle* is
an example. They like one-dimensional characters and
comic-strip-simple settings—Terry Southern's *The Magic
Christian*, and, to much the same extent, *Candy*, are
examples here. They often use a narrative structure that
reflects their disjunctive view of human nature and their
refusal to accept the traditional conception of time. This
is evident in Pynchon's *V* and *Gravity's Rainbow* as well
as in Vonnegut's *Slaughterhouse-Five* and the time-
tripping of Billy Pilgrim. They tend to blur fact and fiction, a tendency arising out of a suspicion that one's
vision of reality is hardly reliable—this is at the center of
Vonnegut's *Breakfast of Champions*. And they utilize a
number of other stylistic devices: self-conscious artifice,
a mocking tone, despair over the possibility of ever cor-
recting human vices, and a tendency to draw imagery
from the more fantastic manifestations of pop culture
(blue movies, Buick LeSabres, Ramada Inns, Big Macs).

It may well be that, as Raymond M. Olderman
maintains, "Black Humor as a term to describe the kind

of comedy used in the fable of the sixties is as good as
any other to explain a phenomenon difficult for most of
us to comprehend. It is a kind of comedy that juxtaposes
pain with laughter, fantastic fact with calmly inadequate
reactions, and cruelty with tenderness. . . ."[4] But behind
most of the stylistic approaches and behind the laughter
is a shared attitude that Vonnegut has perhaps made the
most effective use of—suspicion of easy explanations and
solutions to human problems, and the meaning of existence.

Vonnegut, like most of the other writers who have
been labeled black humorists, is skeptical about the
sufficiency of systems, be they metaphysical, theological,
or psychological, in either comforting us or giving purpose to our lives. He consequently writes, most of the
time, as an observer of the laughable despair that results
from adherence to these systems. Vonnegut's universe is
pluralistic—that is, there is no necessary plan behind it,
no necessary interlocking of its parts according to a single
logical scheme—and the only operative plan for man is
to be ready to be pragmatic, to try out all possibilities
until one that works is found. The difficulty with this
approach to life is that from a cosmic standpoint, all
human responses, since they are based on such a limited
perspective, are laughable.

Vonnegut himself has defined this kind of humor as
gallows humor—the humor of people laughing in the
midst of helplessness. This is humor, he has said, that
"goes against the American storytelling grain. . . . There
is the implication that if you just have a little more en-
ergy, a little more fight, the problem always can be
solved. This is so untrue that it makes me want to cry—
or laugh."[5] Crying will, alas, not help. But laughter
might. For Vonnegut, it is the most effective reaction to
the inevitable frustration of human schemes and desires.
And since laughter is a response to frustration, the big-

gest laughs derive from the biggest fears and disappointments.

A good example of the kind of joke Vonnegut often
deals with is in *Fortitude*, a screenplay for an unproduced
short science-fiction film. Dr. Norbert Frankenstein, in
response to the grief he feels over being unable to save
his mother from cancer, becomes an expert in mechanical
replacements for human organs. When the screen play
opens, he and his assistant, Dr. Tom Swift, are showing a
visiting physician (the *Ladies' Home Journal* Family
Doctor of the Year) around the laboratory.

The visitor soon learns, to his consternation, that Dr.
Frankenstein is keeping a hundred-year-old woman alive
by means of a room full of pumps and pipes and computers. All that remains of Mrs. Lovejoy's original body
is her head, mounted on a tripod, beneath which are two
mechanical arms and a tangle of plumbing. Mrs. Lovejoy
desperately wants to die, but Dr. Frankenstein, who has
told her that she has at least another five hundred years
of life, has rigged her arms so that she cannot feed herself, poison, or turn a gun on herself. His interest in Mrs.
Lovejoy is more than professional, however. He tells her
that when he dies, he will be hooked up to the same machines and that the two of them will enjoy the marriage of
marriages—they will share the same kidney, the same
liver, the same heart. Their moods will always match, her
downs will be his downs, her ups will be his ups. When
she hears this, she pulls out a pistol her beautician has
smuggled to her and shoots him six times.

Twenty-eight minutes later, Dr. Frankenstein's head
is on a tripod beside that of Mrs. Lovejoy. Dr. Swift turns
some dials and shoots the two of them full of martinis
and LSD. As Dr. Frankenstein and his bride blissfully
awaken, a record begins to play. It is Jeanette McDonald
and Nelson Eddy singing "Ah, Sweet Mystery of Life."
The joke, of course, is on Dr. Frankenstein; but it is also

on anyone who hopes that death can be averted by
twentieth-century medicine. Death itself is a bad enough
joke on us; but human schemes to get around it are
worse, as Vonnegut's cosmic irony shows.

Vonnegut's humor points toward mental health,
toward life, and away from insanity and morbidity, even
though in his technique he relies upon repulsive details
and situations and his characters are often deranged. His
purpose seems to be kindness, to help us gain the dignity
that comes from being able to laugh at our own predica-
ment. At the same time, as Vance Bourjaily emphasizes,
Vonnegut, like Lawrence Sterne and Mark Twain, does
not "exempt himself from the humanity whose extrava-
gances and idiocies are on review."[6] His viewpoint is
dictated by the objectivity of his cosmic stance, but this
does not stop him from inserting himself as a character,
or at least a presence, in most of his fiction—and this
makes the beneficent poison in his constant joking easier
to take.

The poison is not so strong in *Player Piano* as it is in
the later novels. But it is there nonetheless, administered
in typical Vonnegut fashion through a narrative that
turns out to be the extended-joke structure Vonnegut returns to again and again.

The central character of *Player Piano* is Paul
Proteus, whose name suggests his discontentment; his
essential nature is changeable, but he lives in an unspecified future time when rampant technology has made
change impossible. American know-how has led to an
anti-utopia, in which machines do nearly all the work,
and the dignity of human labor has been so devalued that
all except the most talented engineers are relegated to
government make-work jobs or to meaningless drill in a
weaponless army.

The Ilium Works is an incredible complex designed
to turn out refrigerators so automatically that the night
shift consists of a single carload of employees. Paul, the

brilliant manager of the Works, is vaguely disturbed by the smugness of his own managerial class and the unhappiness of the disenfranchised workers. Through the influence of a friend, Ed Finnerty, who has quit his prestigious job in Washington to foster revolution, Paul becomes a member of the Ghost Shirt Society, a radical underground Luddite movement that plans to smash the machines and establish a society that would offer satisfying employment for all.

But the joke is on Paul and his cohorts, who had decided that they would make Ilium a laboratory where they would demonstrate how well men could get along with a minimum of machines. They would heat and cook with wood, read books instead of watching TV; it would be a renaissance in upstate New York. As they are touring the city one day, they notice a crowd of people in the waiting room of the railroad station. They discover that the center of attention is a soft-drink machine that had been damaged in the uprising but was now being repaired by a mechanic. Paul realizes that all over the city, workers are instinctively putting back together the machines that had been smashed a few months before. The man repairing the pop machine "was proud and smiling because his hands were busy doing what they liked to do best, Paul supposed—replacing men like himself with machines. He hooked up the lamp behind the Orange-O sign. 'There we are.'" And there Paul and his revolution are—right back at the beginning.

The ending of the novel suggests, of course, the central metaphor of the book: not only has American know-how resulted in a society that is itself a huge player piano, but history is much like the music on a piano roll—it can only repeat itself. Just as Paul finds himself right back where he started, so will all revolutionists and schemers. What is so ironic about the frustration of his plans is that Paul had failed to realize that the very workers he wants to set free by smashing the machines are programmed machines themselves. The essential nature of man may well be protean, and like so many of Vonnegut's characters, Paul is anxious to change himself as well as to change others. He does undergo an inner change, but this has no ultimate impact on external matters. He ends up sadly and comically deluded, however enlightening his experience has been.

Much of the comedy in the novel derives not so much from Paul, however, as it does from the craziness of American society as viewed by a comic outside observer, the Shah of Bratpuhr, who is being taken on a guided tour of the country by a representative of the U.S. State Department. The Shah wants to find out what he can learn from the most technologically advanced nation in the world that would benefit his own backward principality. Naturally, he learns little of benefit as he encounters a soldier who dreams only of the day when he can retire and tell a general off, a housewife who combats boredom by doing the family laundry in the bathtub instead of using her state-provided automatic washer, and a super computer that can answer every question except an ancient riddle of life the Shah puts to it. But Vonnegut has a lot of sport with the translation problems the State Department official encounters in trying to defend American ways against the Shah's shrewd comments.

Unfortunately, Vonnegut's humor does not quite carry *Player Piano*. While the stories of Paul and the Shah complement one another, they do not quite mesh. The Shah remains merely a device (and an old one besides) that enables Vonnegut to work in a commentary on the failures of American democracy. Another problem in the novel is that, even though the book is a warning about mechanization, there is something mechanical about the book itself.

Vonnegut's cosmic irony does, however, serve to bring out one of his major concerns. Like Bernard Malamud in *The Assistant* and John Barth in *The Float-*

ing Opera, Vonnegut is dealing with problems of identity, individuality, and dehumanization. But unlike those of others, Vonnegut's characters are not so much forced into their crises by internal forces as by external ones: automation in *Player Piano*, space travel in *The Sirens of Titan*, Nazism in *Mother Night*, science in *Cat's Cradle*, the power of money in *God Bless You, Mr. Rosewater*, and the fire-bombing of Dresden in *Slaughterhouse-Five*.[7]

An identity fable runs through Vonnegut's fiction and is outlined right at the start. Paul Proteus is troubled by the image of his father, who had been the nation's first National, Industrial, Commercial, Communications, Foodstuffs, and Resources Director, a position actually more important than the presidency of the United States. Paul is expected to live up to that image, but he is not certain that he can, and he eventually decides that he does not want to. But Paul as an American is also troubled by the image of America and the way of life that is forced upon him. He tries to seek a new identity through actions that will also change his country, but he is trapped.

"Partly because there are no escapes within the bounds of normalcy in the real world of the present," Peter J. Reed writes, "Vonnegut's characters frequently talk and act as if they were prisoners. Their being subject to incomprehensible forces in general, and to a social and economic structure which appears overbearing and unresponsive, also contributes to their sense of imprisonment. Cells, small rooms, oubliettes, fences, and prisons abound in the novels, underlying the air of confinement."[8] The fence around the Ilium Works is symbolic of the fence that surrounds Paul's life. He has no more chance to escape than does the cat, early in the novel, who winds up fried on the charged wires.

But while Paul cannot overcome the circumstances of his life, he does, like Lewis's *Babbitt*,[9] enjoy at least a slight victory. The central joke in the novel is at his ex-

pense because of his self-delusion, his belief that he and
his fellow revolutionarists can establish a machineless
agrarian state. When the novel ends, Paul understands
that he has only been fooling himself. The nature of his
identity becomes more clear to him as he raises a bottle
for one last drink with his defeated comrades: " 'To a
better world,' he started to say, but he cut the toast short,
thinking of the people of Ilium, already eager to recreate
the same old nightmare. He shrugged. 'To the record,' he
said, and smashed the empty bottle on a rock." It is here,
where self-delusion becomes the theme and the mode
approaches classical satire, that Vonnegut's comedy cuts
the cleanest and gentlest.

Vonnegut's humor extends in many directions in
Player Piano, however, and Vonnegut certainly relies on
more than just cosmic irony for his effect. But the narrative movement inevitably gathers momentum toward the
depiction of a laughter-provoking catastrophe that is
funny only when viewed from the cosmic vantage point
Vonnegut allows us.

Such humor does not seem very humorous to everybody, however, and the reviews the novel received tended
to reflect this. Charles Lee, for instance, writing in the
Saturday Review of Literature, expressed the opinion
that *Player Piano* "has its bright side as entertainment,
and its witty moments. But it's not funny."[10] Granville
Hicks was able to appreciate Vonnegut as "a sharp-eyed
satirist."[11] But it would be more than a decade and several novels later before Vonnegut's comic vision would
be accepted, if not necessarily understood.

The Sirens of Titan, which appeared seven years
after *Player Piano*, continues many of the same themes
(especially the problem of self-delusion) and employs
some of the same comedy as does Vonnegut's first novel,
but it is a superior work in every respect.

Unlike *Player Piano*, *The Sirens of Titan* is narrated

by a persona who is looking backward from the distant future when men have finally realized that human exploration should be directed inward, that the human soul, not outer space, is the true *terra incognita*. We are told a story set sometime between World War II and what Vonnegut vaguely terms the "Third Great Depression," when men still believed that it was human destiny to push toward the stars.

Malachi Constant, the richest man in the United States, is called to the estate of Winston Niles Rumfoord, who is scheduled to materialize from the "chronosynclastic infundibulum" into which his spaceship plunged while on a journey to Mars. The infundibulum—a gyre-like, intergalactic roller-coaster track on which Rumfoord and his dog, Kazak, are forced to travel around and around and up and down in space and time—enables Rumfoord to see into the future.

Malachi (whose name means "faithful messenger") is told that he will marry Rumfoord's wife, Beatrice, on Mars and that they will conceive a child. From Mars, Malachi will go to Mercury for a time and then return to earth. Eventually he will wind up on Titan, one of the moons of Saturn, with Beatrice and their son. (As characters always do in stories of this sort, both Malachi and Beatrice do what they can to escape the prediction of the oracle. But everything Rumfoord predicts does, of course, come to pass, even though Malachi must discover the details for himself.)

Malachi learns, while on Mars, that Rumfoord is training an army of kidnaped and electronically brainwashed earthlings to return to their mother planet as Martians in a suicidal attack that will serve to unite the warring peoples of earth through the threat of a common enemy. A secondary result of this unification will be the establishment of a new worldwide religion, the Church of God the Utterly Indifferent, based on the frank ac-

ceptance of the idea that God is not a big eye in the sky
watching us, that he does not care at all, and that we are
all simply the victims of accident.

Malachi does not take part in the invasion, however.
He is instead shunted to Mercury, where he spends two
years in a cave. When he does succeed in returning to
earth, he is welcomed as The Space Wanderer, a messiah
whose coming Rumfoord had predicted in founding the
new religion. But—as he does at every turn in the novel
—Malachi soon learns that the joke is on him. In a
symbolic crucifixion/ascension scene, Malachi is sent to
Titan with his wife and son. There he meets Salo, a robot
from the planet Tralfamadore, who has been stranded on
Titan for centuries because of a defective part in his
spacecraft.

It is from Salo that Malachi learns the cruelest joke
of all, that the Tralfamadorians have been directing
human history so that the replacement part, which turns
out to be a good-luck charm Malachi's son has been
wearing around his neck for years, can be delivered to
Titan. Even Rumfoord, who thought he could see everything in the past and future, is under the control of the
Tralfamadorians. And what is the purpose of Salo's mission? What could be so important that the Tralfamadorians would utilize some of the most magnificent achieve-
ments of man to send comforting messages to Salo? (The
Great Wall of China, for example, simply told him to be
patient, the Golden House of Nero meant that they are
doing the best they can for him.) He is carrying a square
of aluminum on which there is a single dot. The meaning
of the dot is Greetings. It is this that Salo is to carry to
the far edge of the universe.

The explanation Salo gives for the purpose of
human history illustrates more clearly than anywhere else
in Vonnegut's work the extent to which his novels are
structured around cosmically ironic jokes. Scholes ex-

plains that "This novel suggests that the joke is on us every time we attribute purpose or meaning that suits us to things which are either accidental or possessed of purpose and meaning quite different from those we would supply."[12] Through the joke, we can also see the extent of Vonnegut's absurdist vision. *The Sirens of Titan* is an expression of the belief that we are imprisoned in a universe that lacks meaning and that there is no way to make sense of the human condition. Even the Tralfamadorian explanation is ultimately inadequate because it raises the larger question of what the Tralfamadorians are for. Who is controlling them?

But despite this statement of human absurdity, the main thrust of Vonnegut's humor is not negative. Vonnegut paradoxically transcends meaninglessness by showing everything as meaningless, thus simultaneously cancelling out both pride and self-pity.[13] In other words, since man is not at the center of creation, he is not responsible for evil. He cannot have fallen (nor can he rise) since there is no place to have fallen *from*. This idea is offered as comfort because it gives us one less reason to feel alienated from ourselves.

Vonnegut's view is that absolute answers are what get people into trouble—trouble that provides him with most of his comic scenes. Accordingly, one of his main themes is the illusions man finds to live by, illusions that fall into two categories.[14]

The first type of illusion is found in both *Player Piano* and *Sirens of Titan*—illusions such as racial and national superiority, social Darwinism, the puritan ethic, and so on, all of which make human existence unnecessarily miserable.

The second kind of illusion, the illusion of a purposeful universe, is, of course, more central to *The Sirens of Titan*. This kind does sometimes work to overcome despair. But it also leads to the formation of dogmatic notions about what the purpose of the universe is. These notions almost always lead, in turn, to inquisitions, witch burnings, and worse things, such as those practiced in Hitler's Germany—one of Vonnegut's main concerns in his next novel, *Mother Night*, published in 1962.

Mother Night, the purported confessions of an American Nazi, is, despite Vonnegut's characteristic debunking tone, one of his grimmest novels in its implications. And it is the only one lacking his fanciful and usually satirical science-fiction devices.

Howard W. Campbell, Jr., a successful playwright in Germany (where he grew up after his father's transfer from the General Electric plant in Schenectady), is persuaded to become an American spy. He infiltrates the Nazi party and becomes a vicious broadcaster of propaganda beamed by German radio at the English-speaking world. But Howard actually is transmitting secret messages to the Allies through a code based on the pause patterns of his speech. His beloved actress wife, Helga, is lost while entertaining troops on the eastern front. After the war is over, Howard surrenders to American forces.

He is quietly allowed to take up residence in New York City's Greenwich Village and lives in seclusion for years. But his identity is eventually discovered. To escape from Israeli agents, who want to try him as a war criminal, he takes refuge in an American Nazi cell, the Iron Guard of the White Sons of the American Constitution.

The Iron Guard mysteriously produces Helga. But Howard learns, in one of the many jokes on him, that the girl is actually Helga's younger sister, Resi. He also learns through Frank Wirtanen, the U.S. Army officer who had persuaded Howard to become an American agent in the first place, that the Iron Guard and Resi are part of a mysterious communist plan to abduct him to Moscow. Resi insists, nonetheless, that she has fallen in love with Campbell, and commits suicide to prove the point.

Wearied by the pressures he has lived under for so long, Howard surrenders to the Israelis and is taken to Jerusalem for trial. Wirtanen is willing to provide evidence of Howard's true role, but Howard hangs himself (or says he will) in his cell. He finds out too late the moral of his life (suggested in Vonnegut's 1966 Introduction to *Mother Night*) that "We are what we pretend to be, so we must be careful about what we pretend to be."

Like Paul Proteus, and to a certain extent Malachi Constant, Howard's problems begin with a kind of willful self-delusion. Despite his success as a playwright, Howard is blind to what is going on around him in the Germany of the 1930s, or at least he chooses to ignore it. He writes nothing but medieval romances, all based on the illusion that life can be given meaning through rescuing a maiden, living up to the code of chivalry, and acting under the twin impulses of love and religious faith in a clearly defined cosmos that is divinely planned and ordered. This would at first seem to be as removed from Nazism as one could get. But, ironically enough, Hitler saw Germany's aggression in terms of a crusade; and he actually had a portrait painted of himself as a questing knight, thus piling illusion upon illusion. So in pretending to ignore Hitler and his programs by writing escape literature, Howard is actually appealing to the spirit of the times. And the very popularity of his plays means that the joke is on him.

On the day he is recruited to become an American agent, he is sitting on a park bench in the Tiergarten in Berlin contemplating his next play, *Das Reich der Zwei*. It is about the love he and his wife have for one another: "It was going to show how a pair of lovers in a world gone mad could survive by being loyal only to a nation composed of themselves—a nation of two." This, as the plot summary of *Mother Night* has already shown, is a hopelessly romantic notion, and the play never gets written. Instead, Howard writes *The Memoirs of a Monoga-*

mous Casanova, a diary of his erotic life with Helga
during the first two years of the war. His intention is to
show the many different ways a married couple could
please one another sexually by assuming numerous roles
(again the matter of identity and illusion). To his laughable outrage, he finds out, after he has been taken to
Jerusalem, that a Russian corporal, an interpreter, obtained a copy of the diary and succeeded in getting it
published in Budapest (with illustrations). It has become
an underground bestseller in the Soviet Union. Again, the
joke is on Howard, and all he can do is rage that "The
part of me that wanted to tell the truth got turned into an
expert liar! The lover in me got turned into a pornogra-
pher! The artist in me got turned into such ugliness as the
world has rarely seen before."

Much of the humor in *Mother Night* turns on just
such compounded absurdity; Vonnegut likes to twist the
knife more than once. A writer such as Terry Southern is
usually equal to Vonnegut in the use of single absurdities,
but Vonnegut's superiority is evident in his ability to
handle multiple layers of dark comicality.[15] A good
example occurs elsewhere in *Mother Night* when Howard
comes home and discovers a hangman's noose left in his
apartment by representatives of the American Legion.
Resi throws the noose into the garbage. The garbage col-
lector actually hangs himself with it because he has discovered a genuine cure for cancer and nobody will listen
to him. Vonnegut piles absurdity upon absurdity until the
noose that symbolizes the punishment Howard deserves
for war crimes he did not commit figures in the self-
destruction of a disappointed trashman.

These layers of absurdity contribute to the depth of
the darkness Vonnegut sees behind human motivation
and the murkiness that surrounds the outcome of all
human events. Try as we will, he seems to say, we can
never escape the darkness that surrounds our every act.
This theme is stated in another way by Mephistopheles in

Goethe's *Faust*: "I am a part of the part that at first was all, part of the darkness that gave birth to light, that supercilious light which now disputes with Mother Night her ancient rank and space, and yet can not succeed." The title of the novel is thus a fitting choice for the story of a man who admits that he "served evil too openly and good too secretly, the crime of his times."

Mother Night may be bleak in its implications, but it is not bleak reading. As Richard Schickel wrote when the book was reissued in 1966, it "is on the contrary, a wonderful splash of bright, primary colors, an artful, zestful cartoon that lets us see despair without forcing us to surrender to it. There is no self-pity at the core of Vonnegut's work, only the purifying laughter of a man who has survived that stage."[16]

Vonnegut's laughter is purifying for reasons outside the larger ones of cosmic irony and multiple layers of absurdity. There are dozens of funny lines, bizarre images, and smart remarks in the novel. Some of the funniest moments involve commentary on writers and writing. Here are two examples. Near the beginning of his confessions, Howard recalls meeting Rudolf Hoess, Commandant of Auschwitz, at a New Year's Eve party in Warsaw in 1943. Hoess suggests that he and Howard collaborate on some stories after the war. "I can talk it," Hoess says, "but I can't write it." Much later, when Howard is in prison in Jerusalem, he receives a note smuggled to him from a prisoner being held in Tel Aviv. The prisoner is Adolf Eichmann, who is writing the story of his life and asks Howard, "Do you think a literary agent is absolutely necessary?" Howard's reply: "For book-club sales in the United States of America, absolutely."

Cat's Cradle abounds in humor of this type partly because the narrator is again a writer, although hardly an author of medieval romances or monogamous pornography. John, a free-lance writer who prefers (for all too

obvious symbolic reasons) to be called Jonah, is re-
searching a book about the sixth of August, 1945, the
day the atomic bomb was dropped on Hiroshima. The
book is to be titled *The Day the World Ended*. His investigation takes him to the laboratory of the late Dr. Felix
Hoenikker, the man who could most fully claim to be the
father of nuclear weapons. He learns that Dr. Hoenikker,
at the time of his death, was trying to discover a way to
make water freeze at a higher temperature—so the Marines could fight on top of mud instead of in it. But Jonah
does not immediately discover whether or not Dr.
Hoenikker was successful.

Some time later, Jonah, in order to write a magazine
article, goes to San Lorenzo, an impoverished Caribbean
island run by Papa Monzano, the chief of state, who is
secretly and mysteriously influenced by Frank Hoenikker,
Dr. Hoenikker's long-vanished son. We eventually learn
that Frank bought favor with Papa by revealing that not
only had Dr. Hoenikker's project succeeded but that
Frank possessed some *ice-nine*, which if released into the
ocean or placed in contact with any water anywhere,
would solidify it instantly. Frank gave Papa a vial of the
substance, which Papa wore on a necklace.

Of course, the inevitable happens. Papa, suffering
horribly from cancer, commits suicide by swallowing the
ice-nine and instantly turning into an *ice-nine* statue. The
next day an airplane crash causes Papa's castle and Papa
himself to slide into the sea. The ocean freezes, and the
sky is filled with tornadoes. Jonah, along with the girl of
his dreams, Mona Aamons Monzano, Papa's adopted
daughter, takes refuge in a bomb shelter. Like so many
other Vonnegut characters, Jonah is thus the victim of an
ironic joke. He sets out to write a book about the day the
world ended, and he winds up living through that day
himself.

San Lorenzo has something stranger than *ice-nine*,
however—the outlawed religion of Bokononism. Its

founder, Bokonon, a black man from Tobago, arrived on San Lorenzo years before as a castaway with Earl Mc-Cabe, a deserter from the United States Marines. The two of them manage to take control of the island. To maintain order and to take the minds of the people off their wretched economic condition, they concoct an ersatz religion based (among other ideas) on translating good vibrations from one believer to another by pressing the soles of the feet together. Bokonon himself lives in the jungle, where he composes the calypsos that comprise Bokononist scripture.

After Jonah emerges from the bomb shelter, he finds that Bokonon is one of the few other survivors. Bokonon hands Jonah a piece of paper on which is written the final sentence for *The Books of Bokonon*: "If I were a younger man, I would write a history of human stupidity; and I would climb to the top of Mount McCabe and lie down on my back with my history for a pillow; and I would take from the ground some of the blue-white poison [the *ice-nine* crystals] that makes statues of men; and I would make a statue of myself, lying on my back, grinning horribly, and thumbing my nose at You Know Who." Jonah's narrative turns out to be just that "history of stupidity." As part of the joke, the metaphoric title he started out with, *The Day the World Ended*, turns out to be literally true.

One of Vonnegut's persistent lessons involves how to take a joke. The conclusion of *Cat's Cradle* certainly presents one of his most graphic illustrations. Just as Bokonon and McCabe have perpetrated a joke on the islanders in their comic scheme for maintaining order through a phony religion, so some greater power has perpetrated a joke on all mankind—the notion that the physical world will remain stable, that water will always solidify at the same temperature, that the climate will always remain hospitable in the warm southern seas. But when all this ceases to be the case, when the punchline is delivered, Bokonon can take the joke because he has enjoyed a few jokes of his own making.

Bokonon, with his religion based on "foma," or harmless lies, is in contrast to Dr. Hoenikker, who is the unwitting cause of the humorous apocalypse with which the novel ends. Vonnegut's scientist, with his childlike inquisitiveness, his inability to respond emotionally to others (one morning he left his wife a tip underneath his breakfast plate), and his amorality ("What is sin?" he asks at one point), is too much a caricature to be taken any way except as a straw man in a rigged sermon. But he is a pivotal figure in the cosmic view of the human condition that Vonnegut is trying to give the reader. Dr. Hoenikker's laboratory is littered with children's puzzles and toys, suggestive of the scientific impulse toward reductionism, the notion that only through concentrated simplification (the movement toward the understanding of basic principles, elemental relationships), can knowledge be advanced. Dr. Hoenikker's mistake is that he chooses not to consider the expanded implications of any of his discoveries. "What hope can there be for mankind," Jonah asks, "when there are such men as Felix Hoenikker to give such playthings as *ice-nine* to such short-sighted children as almost all men and women are?" Bokonon's answer is that there is no hope.

Yet *Cat's Cradle* is ultimately a humane and hopeful novel. "Ironically, its concentrations on the design of the end is a gently humorous program for a new and less pretentious beginning," John R. May writes in his study of the theme of apocalypse in the American novel. "The reasons for its imagined apocalypse are patent: the pastiche of uncontrolled invention and absolutized religion. Bokononism, cutting religion and man down to size, is the contour of our hope. And if the hope is slender, it is nevertheless genuine."[17]

Bokononism, with its cult language of *wrang-wrang*,

karass, vin-dit, wampeter, boko-maru, and *foma,* accounts for much of the popularity *Cat's Cradle* brought
Vonnegut. The language itself is amusing, but it serves to
outline an approach to life that has considerable appeal
as a way of averting catastrophe. Bokononism was born
out of pragmatism and the kind of pop-culture ridicu-
lousness that figures so often in Vonnegut's fiction.
Bokonon (whose real name was Lionel Boyd Johnson,
his initials an oblique suggestion of a conceptual connection involving Lyndon Baines Johnson) concludes, after
reading about the principle of "dynamic tension" (pitting
one muscle against another) promoted by Charles Atlas
in his mail-order body-building school, that the best way
to maintain a humane society on perpetually impoverished San Lorenzo is to artificially establish a state of
dynamic tension between religion and government—
"pitting good against evil, and . . . keeping the tension
between the two high at all times." Bokonon accordingly
arranged that he and his religion be outlawed, and that
those caught practicing it be killed. The resulting tension
gave both Bokononists and government officials a sense of
purpose, something Bokonon considered essential for
happiness and survival.

It is out of this conviction that the more mystical
aspects of Bokononism arise. One of the tenets of the
religion is "that humanity is organized into teams, teams
that do God's Will without ever discovering what they are
doing." The term for each of these teams is *karass.* The
Bokononist spends most of his life trying to discover the
nature of his *karass* and what work it is doing. This is the
process of discovery that is behind the book Jonah
(who reveals himself as a converted Bokononist) writes.

As it turns out, he and Bokonon are on the same
team. But to what purpose? Other than to learn how to
take the ultimate joke, there is no answer. And in the
end, Bokononism, like all systems Vonnegut describes, is

foolish. Bokonon believed that someone was trying to get
him somewhere for some reason, that there is something
special about his own destiny. This, it seems, is an essential mistake; and the result, from Vonnegut's cosmic
viewpoint is inevitably ludicrous. But even though Bokononism is as wrong as the belief of Billy Pilgrim's
mother in the efficacies of gift-shop crucifixes, it is helpful
in that it works to give both Bokonon and Jonah the
dignity they need to take the joke well.

Bokononism and science work against one another in
the book to create dynamic tension of another sort. This
is symbolized by the child's game with string that serves
as the novel's title. One of Dr. Hoenikker's children recalls his disappointment at being shown a cat's cradle by
Dr. Hoenikker and discovering that it does not contain a
cat and is not even a cradle; it is just an arrangement of
string stretched between two hands. The import of the
book is that there are two kinds of cat's cradles—scientific models (the lines, angles, and frame of the string
game suggest this) and philosophical and religious systems. Both are artificial representations of reality. The
question is, which "cradle" is most helpful in promoting
happiness. Vonnegut is clearly on the side of Bokonon
and his *foma*, if for no other reason than that Bokonon
and Vonnegut agree on what must be held sacred: Man
himself.

Another reason for his sympathy with Bokonon is
that Vonnegut, in continuing a line of humor from *Mother
Night*, sees writers as traffickers in helpful lies. Jonah
learns that a writer is a "drug salesman," that perhaps his
most useful purpose is to write "some kind of book to read
to people who are dying or in terrible pain." Later, Jonah
says, "When a man becomes a writer, I think he takes on
a sacred obligation to produce beauty and enlightenment
and comfort at top speed." At no point is truth mentioned;
the comfort of lies in a world of pain is more important.

But while Vonnegut emphasizes the usefulness of

Bokonon's lies, Bokonon is nonetheless a comic figure. "Wherever possible," Jonah writes of Bokonon, "he had taken the cosmic view, had taken into consideration, for instance, such things as the shortness of life and the longness of eternity." The problem is in the "wherever possible." As helpful as Bokononism is, as devoid of false pieties as it is, as concerned as it is with human decency and the necessity of having a sense of purpose, it only enables Jonah to "find some neat way to die." And that seems to be the final message of Bokonon, Vonnegut's most famous messiah, who ends up barefoot, sitting on a rock, and wearing a blue bedspread with blue tufts, his farewell appearance pointing toward Vonnegut's other messiah, the even more ludicrous figure of Eliot Rosewater.

Eliot spends most of his time in *God Bless You, Mr. Rosewater* sitting around in his long underwear in a squalid one-room office in Rosewater, Indiana, where he serves as a combination notary public, volunteer fireman, and comforter of the poor. On the door of his office is a sign, "Rosewater Foundation, How Can We Help You?" And by his cot are two telephones, one of which is red for fire calls. The black one is for calls from the distressed citizens of the surrounding county—from Diana Moon Glampers, "a sixty-eight-year-old virgin who, by almost anybody's standards, was too dumb to live," and who suffers from a paranoid fear of electricity and imagined kidney pains; from a suicidal man who says he "wouldn't live through the next week for a million dollars" but who agrees to go on living when Eliot gets him down to a hundred; from Sherman Wesley Little, an unemployed tool-and-die maker whose second child has cerebral palsy; and from various other people.

Eliot mistakenly believes that these "were the same sorts of people who, in generations past, had cleared the forests, drained the swamps, built the bridges, people whose sons formed the backbone of the infantry in time

of war—and so on." These are the people who are now
forgotten in a money-mad United States, Eliot reasons,
and he tries to help them as best he can. He sometimes
prescribes an aspirin and a glass of wine for his callers.
At other times he advances modest sums of money
known as Rosewater Fellowships. And when those he has
helped want to repay him, he organizes therapeutic fly
hunts in his screenless office.

How Eliot got to be this way is a complicated matter, and the plot structure of *God Bless You, Mr. Rosewater* is extremely complex, perhaps because the central
concern—money as a "psychological germ-carrier"[18]—
affords so many opportunities for humor. "A sum of
money is a leading character in this tale about people,"
Vonnegut writes in his opening sentence, "just as a sum
of honey might properly be a leading character in a tale
about bees." So from the start, Vonnegut sets the novel
up as a fable that moves from lesson to lesson down
through a series of cosmically ironic moral points concerning the insane wisdom of his messianic fool.

The Rosewater Foundation consists of much more
than Eliot's one-room office, and Eliot as president of the
Foundation is much more (or was much more) than his
long johns would indicate. On June 1, 1964, the Rosewater wealth consists of $87,472,033.61, a sum that
produces an income of $3,500,000 a day. Like most
American fortunes of its sort, it was produced through
speculation and bribery during and after the Civil War.
Now channelled into the Rosewater Foundation, the
money is beyond taxation. The oldest son in the direct
line of succession in each generation accedes to the presidency.

From 1947 through 1953, Eliot was a model president. His education at Loomis and Harvard (a doctorate
in international law) was superb. He had served ad-
mirably in Europe during World War II. He had married
a beautiful wife in Paris, Sylvia DuVrais Zetterling. And

he had directed the Foundation money toward research projects in cancer, mental illness, racial prejudice, "and countless other miseries." But then Eliot disappears for a week and crashes a convention of science-fiction writers being held in a motel in Milford, Pennsylvania.

What Eliot admires about science-fiction writers is their cosmic outlook. "The hell with the talented sparrowfarts who write delicately of one small piece of one mere lifetime, when the issues are galaxies, eons, and trillions of souls yet to be born," he says. The science-fiction writer Eliot most admires is Kilgore Trout, the neglected author of eighty-seven paperback books and now, at the age of sixty-six, a stock clerk in a trading-stamp redemption center in Hyannis, Massachusetts. The Kilgore Trout book Eliot most admires is *2BRO2B*, a title that turns out to be the famous question asked by Hamlet. Trout, who is Vonnegut's alter ego (the two full names contain the same number of letters), has as his favorite formula one not unlike Vonnegut's own—to describe a grotesque society and then suggest ways of changing it. In *2BRO2B*, Trout writes about an America, somewhat similar to that of *Player Piano*, in which all the work is done by machines. Because of the eradication of disease, the United States suffers from an overpopulation problem, which is being solved by Suicide Parlors (located at all major intersections). As one of Trout's characters is being eased into death on a Barca Lounger with Muzak in the background, he asks the stewardess who is attending him a central question for both Vonnegut and Eliot, "What in hell are people for?"

Eliot, like most other Vonnegut characters, is in turn forced to ask what *he* is for, a question that is complicated by his past. Eliot is oppressed by the example of his father, Senator Lister Rosewater, who has spent all of his adult life in the Congress of the United States teaching the morality of reactionary Republicanism, a morality of cruelly enforced, repressive laws that is offensive to Eliot.

Eliot is also obsessed with what happened to him during the war when he shot and killed three volunteer firemen (two old men and a fourteen-year old boy) whom he mistook for S. S. troops in a burning building. The incident led to what was diagnosed as battle fatigue and Eliot had to be evacuated to Paris. In addition to all this, Eliot has to cope with his responsibility for the death of his mother in a sailing accident that happened when he was fourteen. As the psychiatrist who treats him after his return from the science-fiction convention (and the several carousing trips that followed) tells Sylvia, "Your husband has the most massively defended neurosis I have ever attempted to treat." The treatment, as one would expect, does not work, and Eliot disappears again.

Ten days later, Sylvia gets a letter from Elsinore, California, where Eliot has gotten involved with the Volunteer Fire Department. It is in this letter that Eliot reveals the flaw that always leads to comedy in a Vonnegut novel. "Maybe I flatter myself when I think that I have things in common with Hamlet," he writes, "that I have an important mission, that I'm temporarily mixed up about how it should be done. Hamlet had one big edge on me. His father's ghost told him exactly what he had to do, while I am operating without instructions." Eliot believes that he is being sent somewhere for some purpose, and, given Vonnegut's omnipresent cosmic perspective, such assumptions can only result in dark comedy.

Unknown to Eliot with his confused sense of mission, there is an intrigue against him. Norman Mushari, a young lawyer whose boyhood idol was Senator Joe McCarthy, has learned one important lesson at Cornell Law School from his favorite professor, Leonard Leech: a lawyer should always be looking for situations where large amounts of cash were about to change hands. Mushari, who learns that the Rosewater Foundation President can be deposed if proved insane, gets an idea. Since Eliot is obviously out of his mind and since Eliot is

the only son of Lister, Mushari persuades Fred Rosewater, the head of another branch of the family, to ini-
tiate a court action that would make the Rosewater
millions his.

This introduces a long subplot involving Fred, a
sexually frustrated life-insurance salesman, his bisexual
wife, Caroline, and the inhabitants of Pisquontuit, Rhode
Island. Among them are the Buntlines, whose ancestors
made a fortune out of a broom factory that employed
disabled Civil War veterans (thus providing Vonnegut
with another case history of wealth). The ironic thing
about Fred's claim to Eliot's position is that the Pisquontuit Rosewaters represent the honest branch of the family. Fred is descended from George Rosewater, the
younger brother of Noah Rosewater, Eliot's direct ances-
tor. Unlike Noah, George did not avoid serving in the
Civil War by buying a substitute. He rose to the rank of
brigadier general and was blinded at Antietam. After the
war, he went east and became a foreman in the Buntline
broom factory.

Meanwhile, Eliot continues his life in Indiana until,
under the pressure of divorce proceedings, he agrees to
go to Indianapolis for a meeting with Sylvia in the hope
of arranging a reconciliation. While reading a Kilgore
Trout novel on the bus, he sees a vision of Indianapolis
in flames, a reminder of the firestorm that followed the
bombing of Dresden, and he passes out. A year later, he
awakens in a mental hospital and learns that he has spent
twelve months playing tennis. Apparently he has recov-
ered from his madness—and just in time, because the
sanity hearing brought on by Mushari and the Pisquontuit Rosewaters is scheduled for the next day. Eliot's
father has hired Kilgore Trout as a consultant, and Trout
wants Eliot to claim that he had been experimenting in
ways to make technologically obsolete people feel loved.
But Eliot gets an idea of his own when he finds out that
Mushari, anxious to discredit him in any way possible,

has bribed people to say bad things about him. As a result, fifty-seven women have brought paternity suits against Eliot—something he is able to turn to his advantage, however. Since Fred would have no chance if Eliot had an heir, Eliot asks that papers be drawn up acknowledging that every child in Rosewater County said to be his *is* his and that they all have the rights of inheritance. Fred Rosewater gets a check for $100,000, and no more. Eliot then proclaims of his "children": "Let their names be Rosewater from this moment on. And tell them that their father loves them no matter what they may turn out to be. And tell them . . . to be fruitful and multiply."

So Eliot has the last laugh on Fred Rosewater and Mushari, but is, in a way, the butt of his own joke. His newly adopted descendants may multiply, and be fruitful in that sense; but the picture Vonnegut has drawn of them in an automated America underscores their uselessness. And how can Eliot love them if he is incapable of loving either his father or his wife? As Vonnegut emphasizes, Eliot had wrecked the life of a woman whose only fault had been that she loved him. Eliot's self-delusion, which reaches its highest point in the godlike conception of himself projected in his final pronouncements, goes back to his essential mistake—that he has an important mission. This, more than his absurd attempts at being a good samaritan, is an indication of his insanity.

But even though he is tripped up at the end, Eliot tries to move toward the cosmic perspective that will lead to sanity. This is evident not only in his interest in science fiction, but is also indicated in an unfinished novel he began on the evening when he first realized that his wife would never come back to him.

Eliot's novel is structured around a reincarnation theme, with human souls returning again and again to earth because heaven is so boring. They have to take their chances on how they will return, however. Kublai

Khan, for instance, is now a veterinarian's wife in Lima, Peru. And Richard the Lion-Hearted is "a pitiful exhibitionist and freelance garbageman in Rosewater, Indiana." But lately, more and more souls do not want to return to earth, even those who had a relatively easy time of it last time around. The narrator of the novel, who was executed as a witch in 1587 in the Austrian village of Dillingen, and who herself has had no burning desire to take her chances in this world again, decides to seek another incarnation to find out what horrible thing has been happening of late to the reborn souls on earth. When the novel breaks off, she has learned that she is to be sent to Rosewater.

Here Eliot tries for the long view of the centuries and an outside perspective on human life. He does come up with an answer to the problems of dislocation and depersonalization that plague him, one that seems workable to him.

This answer is presented in the baptismal prayer he says over a set of twins born to Mary Moody, one of the useless nobodies he tries to help: "God damn it, you've got to be kind."

Vonnegut thus strikes an uncertain balance between the cosmic and the pragmatic in his characterization of Eliot Rosewater, and the result is his most thoroughly funny novel. "It's a tribute to Kurt Vonnegut, Jr.," Daniel Talbot wrote in his review of the book, "that he has covered such a large territory of human follies in so short a book . . . the author has literally taken on the late Norbert Wiener's book title—*The Human Use of Human Beings*—and fashioned a black satire out of its implications. His technique of presenting this material is fascinating—an amalgam of short comic strip-like takes, dada dialogue . . . no characterization, minimal plot, and straight dramaturgy. The net effect is at once explosively funny and agonizing."[19]

The explosiveness, if not the agony, of Vonnegut's

humor also extends into the thinly and somewhat strangely veiled topical satire on the 1964 Republican presidential candidate, Barry Goldwater, whose name and family background of wealth as well as his political conservatism, are satirized in the depiction of Senator Lister Rosewater.

But as funny as *God Bless You, Mr. Rosewater* is, it is not a well-structured novel. There is an awkward movement from the present to the past as Vonnegut fills the reader in with the Rosewater family history, and the focus on Eliot and his problems is lost when Fred Rosewater's story is told. There is a problem too in Eliot's response to his wartime experience. His adulation of volunteer firemen and his conception of the earth as a planet with an atmosphere that, because of its oxygen, "was eager to combine violently with almost everything the inhabitants held dear" is comic in a pathetic way. But this obsession somehow does not seem to be a satisfactory response to the trauma that triggered it in the burning building during the war. Vonnegut's next novel, *Slaughterhouse-Five*, which features Eliot Rosewater and Kilgore Trout as well as Howard W. Campbell, Jr., is a corrective on this point.

Slaughterhouse-Five is several stories in one, all told simultaneously. The main part of the novel deals with the central character, Billy Pilgrim, what happens to him during the Battle of the Bulge, how he survives the fire-bombing of Dresden, and how he leads his life after World War II. In those postwar years he becomes a successful optometrist and imagines he travels by flying saucer to the planet Tralfamadore. But it is also the story of Vonnegut himself and his experiences at Dresden and what happened to him afterward. In addition, it is a story about the difficulty of writing a novel that deals adequately with the horror of our times. It is with this problem that Vonnegut begins.

The book starts and ends with an autobiographical frame. Vonnegut explains that ever since the late 1940s he has been telling people that he has been working on a book about Dresden. He lived through the surprise raid on what was assumed to be a safe city. Since it contained few targets of military importance, it was assumed that Dresden would not be massively bombed. As a consequence, its population had been doubled by prisoners of war and by refugees from the eastern front. But on the night of February 13, 1944, eight-hundred Royal Air Force Lancaster bombers, striking in waves, dropped high-explosive bombs followed by over 650,000 incendiaries, causing a firestorm that could be seen more than two hundred miles away. On February 14, American B-17 Fortresses carried out a second raid, followed by P-51 Mustang fighters, which completed the destruction of the city with strafing missions. The official death count is the figure 135,000 listed by the Dresden police chief. But some estimates indicate that more than 200,000 people were either killed outright, burned to death during the conflagration, or died afterward. Vonnegut, a prisoner of war like Billy Pilgrim, was herded with other POWs into the underground cold-storage area of a slaughterhouse, and emerged after the raid to see the city looking like the face of the moon. Vonnegut tried to obtain the air force report on the raid when he wanted to begin writing about Dresden, but he was told that the information was still classified.[20]

Being denied access to the report was not the main problem for Vonnegut in writing the book, however. And, in a sense, he was able to begin work on it long before *Slaughterhouse-Five* materialized. As Jerome Klinkowitz has pointed out, the matter of Dresden furnished the informing principle for *Player Piano, Mother Night*, and *God Bless You, Mr. Rosewater*.[21] But until *Slaughterhouse-Five*, Vonnegut was not able to deal with

Dresden directly, and he was not able to come up with an approach that would work to exorcise what had become his private demon.

His first step in coming up with that approach was to visit an old friend, Bernard V. O'Hare, who had been with him at Dresden. O'Hare's wife, as Vonnegut recounts in his opening frame, was suspiciously hostile to the projected book because she feared that what he wanted to do was to write a novel glorifying war, something that John Wayne and Frank Sinatra could star in when it was made into a movie. The truth of the matter, she points out, was that Vonnegut, O'Hare, and most of the other men actually involved in the war were little more than children at the time. "So then I understood," Vonnegut writes. "It was war that made her so angry. She didn't want her babies or anybody else's babies killed in wars. And she thought wars were partly encouraged by books and movies." Vonnegut calms her down by telling her that he will subtitle the book, "The Children's Crusade," after the infamous idea, concocted in 1213 by two monks, to raise armies of children in France and Germany, march them to North Africa, and sell them as slaves (30,000 children were actually recruited—half got to North Africa and were sold, most of the others drowned on the way).

Vonnegut later recounts how he receives a Guggenheim Fellowship and returns to Dresden with O'Hare. They make friends with a cab driver who takes them to the slaughterhouse. The driver sent O'Hare a postcard the next Christmas, writing "I wish you and your family also as to your friend Merry Christmas and a happy New Year and I hope that we'll meet again in a world of peace and freedom in the taxi cab if the accident will." The phrase, "if the accident will," determines the order of events and their significance in the novel. As much as Vonnegut would like to see order and significance in what happened at Dresden and afterward, it all comes down to a matter of accidents—some fortuitous, most not. All the accidents, from school girls being boiled alive in a water tower to the assassinations of Martin Luther King and Robert Kennedy, are followed by the catchphrase, "So it goes."

Vonnegut also recounts how, to kill some time while in a motel room, he looked through the Gideon Bible for tales of destruction. There he read the passage in Genesis about God raining fire and brimstone on Sodom and Gomorrah and Lot's wife being turned to a pillar of salt when she looked back as she and her husband were fleeing the condemned cities. Vonnegut says that in looking back at Dresden, he too has been turned into a pillar of salt, that perhaps the essential mistake is to try to account for what had happened. There is no way that he, as a participant, can obtain the cosmic view necessary for clarification or even for coherence. So Vonnegut tells the story of Billy Pilgrim by haphazardly moving back and forth in time and concentrating on the accidents that make up the extended dark joke of the Children's Crusade that World War II is for Billy.

Billy was born in 1922 (the same year as Vonnegut), and, like most other Vonnegut protagonists, is in conflict with his father. (His father once tried to teach him to swim by throwing him into a swimming pool and letting him sink. Billy's father was later shot and killed on a deer-hunting trip.) Billy does poorly in college, enters the army, and becomes a chaplain's assistant—a service assignment that establishes Billy as a Christ figure, a symbolic connection that is maintained throughout the rest of the narrative. He is stranded behind enemy lines during the Battle of the Bulge, and, along with a tank gunner named Roland Weary, is captured and marched toward Germany. Billy and Weary are eventually loaded into a boxcar with a crowd of other prisoners and begin rolling eastward. Weary dies of gangrene on the journey and irrationally blames Billy for his fate. Paul Lazzaro, a

vicious paranoid who believes Weary to be his only
friend, vows to kill Billy.

The prisoners are taken to a camp in Germany
where they are greeted by a group of British officers.
They are well-fed and in good health because, through an
error, they are receiving five hundred Red Cross packages
a month instead of the fifty they are supposed to get. The
British prisoners-of-war give Billy and his fellow prisoners a big welcome dinner and put on a show for them—
all of which so overwhelms Billy that he winds up in sick
quarters. A few days later the Americans are marched to
Dresden, where they are put to work bottling a vitamin
supplement for pregnant women and are housed in
slaughterhouse number five. Howard W. Campbell, Jr.,
shows up and tries to talk them into joining the Free
America Corps and help the Germans fight the Russians.
The Dresden raid ends all such talk, however, and Billy
and his comrades are subsequently put to work "mining"
bodies in the devastated city. It is here that the most
horrible joke in the novel is told. A schoolteacher named
Edgar Derby takes a teapot from the ruins and is arrested for plundering. "I think the climax of the book will
be the execution of poor old Edgar Derby," Vonnegut
tells O'Hare in the prefatory chapter. "The irony is so
great. A whole city gets burned down, and thousands and
thousands of people are killed. And then this one American soldier is arrested in the ruins for taking a teapot.
And he's given a regular trial, and then he's shot by a
firing squad."

Billy returns to Ilium, New York, after the war ends
and marries the daughter of the founder of the optometry
school in which he enrolls. Billy and his wife have two
children, one of whom becomes a Green Beret and fights
in Vietnam. Billy's business prospers and he drives a
Cadillac with John Birch Society stickers on its rear
bumper. But he has gotten so addicted to becoming "unstuck in time," as a consequence of his war experiences

that, at one point, he has himself committed to a mental hospital. There he meets Eliot Rosewater and through him becomes acquainted with the novels of Kilgore Trout. Later he meets Trout and invites him to his eighteenth wedding anniversary. Trout shows up, and, "gobbling canapes . . . talking with a mouthful of Philadelphia cream cheese and salmon roe," is the hit of the party.

Obviously influenced by the novels of Trout, Billy imagines, on the night of his daughter's wedding in 1967, that he is kidnapped by a Tralfamadorian flying saucer and taken to a zoo on Tralfamadore. There he is mated with Montana Wildhack, a Hollywood sex symbol whose mysterious disappearance had been played up in the news. Billy and Montana lead an almost idyllic life and have a baby. But the most significant thing that happens to Billy on Tralfamadore is that his captors explain their concept of time to him.

While still in the flying saucer, Billy asks where he is and how he got there. "It would take another Earthling to explain it to you," says a voice from a speaker on the wall. "Earthlings are the great explainers, explaining why this event is structured as it is, telling how other events may be achieved or avoided. . . . All time is all time. It does not change. It does not lend itself to warnings or explanations. It simply *is*. Take it moment by moment, and you will find that we are all, as I've said before, bugs in amber."

The Tralfamadorians add that all moments exist simultaneously, hence nothing can be done to change the past or the future because, technically, there is neither past nor future. When someone is dead, it simply means that he is in a bad condition at that moment but that at another moment he is alive and well and possibly happy. There is thus no such thing as free will, and the best Billy can do is to accept the message inscribed on the locket that dangles between Montana's breasts (and is also displayed on a wall plaque in his office on earth): "God grant me the serenity to accept the things I cannot change, courage to change the things I can, and wisdom always to tell the difference."

Billy gets back to earth and survives an airplane crash only to learn that his wife has died of carbon-monoxide poisoning. When he gets out of the hospital, he succeeds in getting on radio talk-shows to tell what he has learned from the Tralfamadorians. He eventually becomes famous and is in demand as a speaker, giving speeches (after the manner of Vonnegut himself) on space travel and Tralfamadorian time theory. On the twenty-first anniversary of the Dresden raid, he is gunned down by a hired killer while speaking in a Chicago arena. The paranoid friend of Roland Weary, Paul Lazaro, is responsible.

The novel ends with Vonnegut, after mentioning the recent deaths of Martin Luther King and Robert Kennedy, musing about what the Tralfamadorians taught Billy. "If what Billy Pilgrim learned from the Tralfamadorians is true," Vonnegut writes, "that we will all live forever, no matter how dead we may sometimes seem to be, I am not overjoyed. Still—if I am going to spend eternity visiting this moment and that, I'm grateful that so many of those moments are nice." Vonnegut is, as the events recounted in the novel surely indicate, being sarcastic here. And what he does is to make his "famous book about Dresden" into something of a shaggy-dog story with a horrible twist—if we all live forever, so too will the fire-bombing of Dresden go on forever.

But even though this is the cosmic implication of what Billy learns and Vonnegut posits, Tralfamadorian time theory does have pragmatic value in dealing with the crises they have both been through. What Billy does in his imagined travels to Tralfamadore is what Kilgore Trout and the other science-fiction writers do—that is, to try "to re-invent themselves and their universe," to come up with some new lies so they can go on living. Billy is unhinged to the point of madness by what happens to him in the war, and he can no longer control his time-tripping, so he invents the Tralfamadorians to make his madness accord with some vision of reality. His life is thus given a certain order and pattern and he does attain "serenity." But how seriously does Vonnegut take this and what practical value does it have for him? Here is a significant statement: "When I think about my own death," he writes, "I don't console myself with the idea that my descendants and my books and all that will live on. Anybody with any sense knows that the whole solar system will go up like a celluloid collar by-and-by. I honestly believe, though, that we are wrong to think that moments go away never to be seen again. This moment and every moment lasts forever."[22]

Vonnegut apparently takes Billy seriously as a messiah, as a bringer of a message that can be applied to the question of how to deal with catastrophe and go on living. Vonnegut's seriousness is indicated in the large number of parallels he draws between Billy and Christ. Roland Weary makes Billy into a scapegoat, and he is reviled by the other prisoners while on the journey to the prisoner-of-war camp. He is forced to stand up most of the way, hanging from a crossbar in the boxcar. And, two days after the war ends, he is sleeping, still in Dresden, when he is slowly awakened by the sound of a man and a woman speaking in German somewhere nearby. "Before Billy opened his eyes," Vonnegut writes, "it seemed to him that the tones might have been those used by the friends of Jesus when they took His ruined body down from His cross. So it goes."

Even though Billy is a comic figure in many scenes, he is nowhere near as ludicrous as Eliot Rosewater in the role of messiah. Billy has more to say than simply, "God damn it, you've got to be kind." He says you've got to

reinvent yourself and your universe. As Scholes wrote in
his review of *Slaughterhouse-Five*, "Only Billy's time-
warped perspective could do justice to the cosmic absurdity of his life, which is Vonnegut's life and our
lives."[23]

But, as do all of Vonnegut's protagonists, Billy
nonetheless lives a life that is an extended joke. Like all
of them, he is comic because he is a victim of his illusions. We know that Tralfamadore does not exist and
that Montana Wildhack is just a dream. His life is a
series of accidents, most of which can only be seen as
manifestations of some grotesquely sick sense of humor
that is behind it all (although this too is an illusion).
What should we expect of Billy when he regains consciousness as the sole survivor of an airplane crash and
learns of his wife's absurd death but that he gets himself
on crackpot talk-shows? He is crazy, an unwitting clown,
and it is only fitting that a maniac should arrange his
assassination.

Yet Billy is the character toward whom Vonnegut
worked ever since Paul Proteus; he is the one central
character who is able to be protean, to successfully
change himself for survival. At the end of the novel,
O'Hare tells Vonnegut that by the year 2000, the world's
population will double to seven billion people. Vonnegut
replies sarcastically, "I suppose they will all want dignity." They most certainly will, and one way they may
find it is through the example of Billy Pilgrim. Or, to
repeat what Vonnegut said in his 1973 *Playboy* interview, "It may be that the population will become so
dense that *everybody's* going to live in ugliness, and that
the intelligent solution—the only possible solution—will
be to change our insides."[24] And that is just what Billy
does, fool though he may be, messiah that he is—he
rescues himself and arranges his resurrection through a
work of his own imagination, a rationalizing fantasy.

Near the conclusion of his preface to *Slaughterhouse-*

Five, Vonnegut states that "I've finished my war book now. The next one I write is going to be fun!" The next one turned out to be *Breakfast of Champions*, and it does turn out to be fun even though it is, like *Slaughterhouse*, a partially autobiographical, partially therapeutic work, that has its basis in manic depression, and, in its own way, is a rationalizing fantasy of another sort.

Breakfast of Champions has its genesis in Vonnegut's efforts at dealing with his own self-acknowledged manic-depressive tendencies. In the late 1960s, he was suffering from periodic fits of depression. His doctor prescribed Ritalin, an amphetamine, and Vonnegut's depression lifted. "I used to think I was responding to Attica or to the mining of Haiphong," he said. "But I wasn't. I was obviously responding to internal chemistry. All I had to do was take one of these little pills."[25] This experience impressed Vonnegut with the degree to which human motivation and behavior is influenced by physiological factors, how a pill no larger than the head of a pin can alter personality.

The cosmic view that thus emerges in *Breakfast of Champions* is based on the idea, hinted at but not very fully explored in the earlier novels, that we are robots or machines made up of rubbery tubes with boiling chemicals inside. In the opening section of *Breakfast of Champions*, Vonnegut writes that "it is a big temptation to me, when I create a character for a novel, to say that he is what he is because of faulty wiring, or because of microscopic amounts of chemicals which he ate or failed to eat on that particular day." The hitch is (as in *Slaughterhouse-Five*) that Vonnegut has to look at himself as a chemically fueled machine when he enters the novel as a fellow "character," programed the same way the other people in the book are. This can hardly be an upbeat approach to one's depression, and Vonnegut admits that "suicide is at the heart of the book."[26] But at the same time, Vonnegut manages to find a pragmatic solution that makes it possible for him to go on living even if it is not true and even if it makes himself into a comic figure.

Vonnegut begins *Breakfast of Champions* by indicating he is writing the novel as a fiftieth birthday present for himself, trying to clear his head of "all the junk in there" by getting rid of the characters that have been haunting him for years. What he does is to contrive a meeting between Kilgore Trout and Dwayne Hoover, a middle-aged Pontiac dealer in Midland City who is suffering from a brain full of bad chemicals.

Although he does not know it, Dwayne is about to go berserk. A major cause will be the ideas he learns from one of Trout's novels, *Now It Can Be Told*. The core of these ideas is that the reader of the book is the only creature in the universe who has free will. All other creatures are robots (a common fantasy, by the way, that occurs in exaggerated form among paranoid schizophrenics). At the end of *Breakfast of Champions*, Dwayne suffers from the same delusion that other deluded Vonnegut characters do—the idea that he is unique, the idea that his life must be something special, the idea that he alone has some purpose to fulfill. Given Vonnegut's cosmic viewpoint, whatever Dwayne does and why he does it under this delusion is the stuff of comedy because he makes the mistake that he and he alone has free will—a laughable assumption for any character in a Vonnegut novel to make.

What brings Trout and Dwayne together is an invitation Trout receives to speak at a festival celebrating the opening of the Mildred Barry Memorial Center for the Arts in Midland City. Trout has been invited upon the recommendation of Eliot Rosewater (who else?), who agrees to loan the Center an El Greco worth three million dollars if the chairman of the festival will hire Trout as a speaker. Trout, whose novels are still being published as filler material in pornographically illustrated books and magazines, is living in a basement apartment in Cohoes, New York, and working as an installer of combination storm windows when he gets the letter from Midland City and a check for a thousand dollars.

Trout goes to Manhattan (with half of his honorarium pinned to his underpants) to look through the porno shops for some of his novels to take along. (His publishers never bother to send his complimentary copies.) He is mugged on a handball court underneath the Queensboro Bridge on Fifty-ninth Street and loses all but ten dollars of his travel fund. He is forced to hitchhike west, getting a ride in a truck that is hauling 78,000 pounds of Spanish olives. Trout talks to the truck driver about conservation, politics, friendship in the modern world, and aluminum siding.

Meanwhile Dwayne is becoming increasingly insane. He sees a monstrous duck directing traffic. He sees eleven moons in the sky. He insults his sales manager, Harry LeSabre (who wrongly suspects that Dwayne knows of his fondness for dressing up in women's clothing on weekends). Dwayne goes home and puts the muzzle of a .38-calibre revolver into his mouth. Then, on second thought, he decides to shoot the flamingo on his bathtub enclosure instead. He goes out, gets into a black Plymouth Fury he had taken in trade, and drives crazily to the new Holiday Inn, of which he is part owner. He climbs the stairs to the roof of the motel and stands there, asking himself where he is. He has forgotten almost everything; he has even forgotten that his wife had killed herself by eating Drano and that his son, Bunny, who plays piano in the cocktail lounge of the Inn, is one of the most notorious homosexuals in Midland City.

The conversation between Trout and the truck driver continues on through Pennsylvania and West Virginia as Vonnegut describes the landscape of a dying planet—topsoil gone, hillsides collapsing into the strip-mine pits, and rusted Cadillacs capsized in muddy creeks.

Dwayne's chemicals, meanwhile, are seething. He develops echolalia and compulsively repeats the last word of whatever he has just heard: "When the radio said that there had been a tornado in Texas, Dwayne said this out loud: 'Texas.'" And he reacts like a coiled rattlesnake when he incorrectly concludes that his receptionist and mistress, Francine Pefko, is being nice to him only so she can sweet-talk him into buying her a Colonel Sanders Kentucky Fried Chicken franchise. (What she actually longs for is radial tires for her car.)

Trout finally arrives in Midland City, enjoying the last leg of his journey in a Ford Galaxie (he asks the driver what it is like to steer something a hundred-thousand light years in diameter). Dwayne is sitting in the cocktail lounge of the Holiday Inn on a zebra-skin banquette as Bunny plays the piano. Another person, Vonnegut himself, is looking on through the silvered lenses of one-way sunglasses. Vonnegut is drinking a Black and White and water and mouthing the word *schizophrenia*. When the cocktail waitress brings Dwayne his drink, a House of Lords martini, she makes her customary remark, "Breakfast of Champions," a remark that often accompanies the serving of drinks in the midwest.

Dwayne is hoping that the artists who have come to Midland City for the festival will tell him some new truths about life that will enable him to keep out of the mental ward of the Midland County Hospital. Rabo Karabekian, the "minimalist" painter, whose work, *The Temptation of St. Anthony*, consisting of a vertical stripe of orange reflecting tape on a field of green wall paint, delivers a lecture that would seem to offer some hope for Dwayne.

Sensing antagonism toward him in the cocktail lounge when he enters (he had been paid fifty-thousand dollars for *The Temptation of St. Anthony*) Karabekian defends his masterpiece. It shows all that is important about life, he argues; it represents the "I am" in every animal, the receptor to which all messages from the outside are sent. "It is unwavering and pure, no matter what preposterous adventure may befall us," Karabekian says. "A sacred picture of St. Anthony alone is one vertical, unwavering band of light. If a cockroach were near him or a cocktail waitress, the picture would show two such bands of light. Our awareness is all that is alive and maybe sacred in any of us. Everything else about us is dead machinery." Karabekian's words cause Vonnegut, who has suicidally come to the conclusion that we are all just machines doomed to collide with one another repeatedly, to feel himself "born again." But Dwayne Hoover gains nothing from the lecture; he sits hypnotized by the beads of lemon oil on the surface of his martini.

When Trout shows up carrying a copy of *Now It Can Be Told*, Dwayne's hypnotized eyes fix on him. Dwayne staggers up to Trout and asks for a message. He sees the novel, grabs it, and begins to speed-read it. His reaction to the news that he is "an experiment by the Creator of the Universe" and that he is the only person in the cocktail lounge or anywhere else not to be a robot, "the only creature in the entire Universe who has free will," is to walk over to his son at the piano and to pound Bunny's head up and down the keyboard. Then he socks the cocktail waitress, runs across the street to his Pontiac showroom and breaks Francine Pefko's jaw and three ribs. As he continues his rampage, he bites off the topmost joint of Trout's ring finger and assaults more than a dozen other victims. Vonnegut tries to stay out of his way, but someone else jumps back and breaks Vonnegut's watch crystal and his big toe. Two state policemen eventually subdue Dwayne on the median of the Interstate highway and haul him off to jail. The resulting lawsuits will bankrupt him and he will wind up on Midland City's skid row, Vonnegut tells us.

In the epilogue to the novel, Vonnegut rents a

Plymouth Duster from Avis and goes to intercept Trout as the science-fiction writer returns from the hospital where he had his finger bandaged up. Vonnegut parks the car near the supply yard of the Maritimo Brothers Construction Company and gets out to wait. Vonnegut suddenly sees a huge Doberman pinscher leaping at him from behind the supply-yard fence. Vonnegut, for all his being born again through his new conception of himself as an unwavering band of light, reacts like a machine. A message is sent from his eyes to his brain, which in turn contacts the hypothalamus, and on down the chain of switches and reactions until he receives a massive charge of adrenaline. He retracts his testicles into his abdominal cavity and leaps over his car. The dog hits the fence and is thrown back. The joke this time is on the author. He can no more control his responses than can the characters in his novel.

Trout, who watches all of this, starts to run away. Vonnegut chases him and tells him that he is only a character in a book and that his creator will reward him for all his suffering with the Nobel Prize for Medicine. "I am approaching my fiftieth birthday, Mr. Trout," Vonnegut anxiously explains. "I am cleansing and renewing myself for the very different sorts of years to come. Under similar spiritual conditions, Count Tolstoi freed his serfs. Thomas Jefferson freed his slaves. I am going to set at liberty all the literary characters who have served me so loyally during my writing career." He adds that Trout is to be the only character so informed, and Trout, ironically, is stuck with the burden that destroys character after character in Vonnegut's novels—the burden of being told he has free will even though Vonnegut again and again demonstrates the impossibility of the very concept. As Vonnegut somersaults into the void, he hears Trout's distant voice requesting only one thing—to be made young.

Several layers of irony thus run through the novel and the humor is compounded many times. Vonnegut shows Dwayne going insane while Vonnegut cuts back and forth from the zany adventures and conversations of the world's most neglected writer making his way west. The climactic confrontation becomes all the more comic when Dwayne grabs Trout's schizophrenic novel and thinks *Now It Can Be Told* is a message intended for him alone. But Trout and Dwayne are not the only ones suffering from delusion, the delusion that they are not machines and that they may act as they wish. When Vonnegut enters the story, we soon learn that he is as deluded as the rest. He feels that he is a new person after Karabekian's speech, but then he reacts mechanistically when the dog jumps at him. Again the point is that any comforting assumption or belief, even Vonnegut's own, is laughable when looked at cosmically. But as false as it is shown to be, Karabekian's message does have pragmatic value—it does help Vonnegut (the character, at any rate) deal with his schizophrenia, even if it does not keep him from being a comic figure.

Karabekian's ideas, however central they are to Vonnegut's vision, no more oppressively dominate *Breakfast of Champions* than does the manic wisdom of Eliot in *God Bless You, Mr. Rosewater*, the only other Vonnegut novel that is funnier. The extended cosmic jokes (and especially the central one on Vonnegut) are there, but much of the humor in *Breakfast of Champions* derives from Vonnegut's synopses of Trout stories and various gag situations. There is also the matter of Vonnegut's illustrations, made with a felt-tip pen and included as if the audience has lost the ability to read. (It is significant that Trout is to take part in a seminar on the American novel and its future in the age of McLuhan.) The illustrations also suggest that the book is intended as an artifact, as something of a Rosetta Stone with its pictures of beaver, hamburgers, and Volkswagens, to be discovered by explorers from another planet long after the earth is dead.

Much of Vonnegut's comedy is also aimed at Midland City with its Sacred Miracle Cave and its Cathedral of Whispers (in which thousands of people have been married), its white boulder painted to resemble Moby Dick, and a skeleton said to be the remains of Jesse James. Vonnegut's emphasis on such bizarre Americana and all of the insanity in the flatlands can only remind one of Sherwood Anderson's *Winesburg, Ohio*, or Hamlin Garland's *Main-Travelled Roads*, or sections of Vonnegut's fellow Indianapolitan, Booth Tarkington. Vonnegut depicts the midwest, a region of supposed conservatism and sanity, as a place of madness. But it is only by returning to such a place to face his past and his own self-destructive impulses that Vonnegut can himself be freed. At the end, he holds a mirror up to his eye (Trout thinks mirrors are *leaks* into another universe) and sees a single teardrop falling—a tear of sadness, a tear of relief, and a tear of laughter all in one, the Vonnegut response to the terrors that surround us all.

The same terrors and the same response are present in *Slapstick*, a work that seems more an afterthought than an important novel, despite Vonnegut's claim in the prologue that it is the closest he will ever come to writing an autobiography. The book is dedicated to Laurel and Hardy by way of explaining the title. Life, Vonnegut points out, is a slapstick comedy based on a "fundamental joke." The joke comes out of constantly being asked to do our best at all times and then bungling everything because of our limited agility and intelligence. Vonnegut knows this joke well, he writes, because he "was so perpetually intoxicated and instructed by Laurel and Hardy" when he was growing up during the great depression. He also knows it because of the unfortunate example of his sister, Alice, who died of cancer at the age of forty-one, two days after her husband had been killed in a train wreck. Four children, the youngest only a year old, were orphaned. "Soap opera!" Alice had said in commenting on her life. "Slapstick."

Vonnegut's relationship with his sister was close, and he confesses that she is the audience he has been writing for all along. Out of this relationship comes a dream that occurs as Vonnegut is flying to an uncle's funeral in Indianapolis with his older brother, Bernard. The dream provided Vonnegut with the story he eventually turned into *Slapstick*.

The hero-narrator of the novel, which opens in Vonnegut's typically indefinite future, is Dr. Wilbur Daffodil-11 Swain, the final (as well as the tallest) President of the United States, sitting in a clearing in a jungle on Manhattan Island. He is wearing a purple toga made from draperies that once hung in the Americana Hotel. The bridges to the mainland are down, the tunnels are blocked, and the island is a quarantine area because of a mysterious plague known as the Green Death.

Wilbur then tells us his story. He and his twin sister, Eliza, were mistaken for Mongolian idiots when they were born, and they were isolated by their parents (the father a Mellon, the mother a Rockefeller) in a mansion near Galen, Vermont. But the twins are actually a new type of human being, "Neanderthaloids," over seven feet tall by the age of ten with twelve fingers, twelve toes, and four nipples each. They are also supremely intelligent. But their most important characteristic is that they "were born with the capacity and the determination to be utterly happy all the time." Given Vonnegut's cosmic irony, his sense of slapstick, such a capacity is bound to lead to trouble—and it does.

Wilbur and Eliza can only be happy when they are together, and they can think as geniuses only when their

heads are within a few feet of each other. They are sep-
arated for their education, however, and except for a few
encounters that turn out to be more traumatic than
happy, circumstance forces Wilbur and Eliza to remain
apart for the rest of their lives. Eliza is locked up for
many years in an institution for the feeble-minded (as
brilliant as she is, she is unable to read or write). She
somehow manages to obtain a lawyer (Norman Mushari,
Jr., from *God Bless You, Mr. Rosewater*), sue her family
for damages, buy half-interest in the New England Patri-
ots of the National Football League, and move into a
condominium in Machu Picchu, the ancient Inca capital
in Peru.

Wilbur goes to Harvard Medical School and then
becomes a practitioner of rural medicine. He runs for
Senator from Vermont and even becomes President,
proposing a scheme for happiness that he and Eliza
thought up when they were children. They concluded that
American society is a cold and unhappy one because
nobody has enough relatives any more. The solution,
which has been alluded to in chapter one, is to assign
everyone thousands of relatives by computer. Each
American will get a new middle name and number. The
middle name—Daffodil or Chipmunk or Peanut or
whatever—would indicate the artificial extended family.
The number would indicate individual relationships
within the family—two people with the same number
would be siblings, those with different numbers would be
cousins. Wilbur's campaign button reads, "Lonesome No
More."

But because there are complications beyond Wilbur's control, and because of his limited agility and intelligence, "Lonesome No More" (like all of the comic
schemes for happiness Vonnegut satirizes) does not get
much of a chance to work out.

By the time Wilbur is elected, the United States has
so far exhausted its resources that the harbors are used

mainly by sailing ships and the farmwork is being done
with horses. There is so little fuel left to run the gener-
ators that Wilbur is forced to raid the National Archives
for paper to burn in the power plants so that the computers can be used to put "Lonesome No More" in oper-
ation. He starts with the documents from the Nixon
administration, then he moves on to those of the Grant
and Harding administrations. The middle names do get
assigned, however, and Wilbur believes that Americans
are happier than ever. But then people begin to die of the
Green Death and another ailment called the Albanian
Flu. The United States breaks up into the "Kingdom of
Michigan" and various territories controlled by the
armies of such upstarts as the "Duke of Oklahoma."

There are some foreign problems as well. The Chinese have created millions of geniuses by teaching groups
of telepathically congenial specialists to think as one
mind. The Chinese learn how to miniaturize themselves
to save resources, carrying out the process until they become microscopic—and this, it turns out, is the cause of
the Green Death. The Chinese, "who were peace-loving
and meant no one any harm," Vonnegut explains, "were
nonetheless invariably fatal to normal-sized human beings when inhaled or ingested."

The Albanian Flu is also blamed on the Chinese,
who have developed a way of sending people to Mars
without using a space vehicle. The flu germs are Martians
who are brought to earth on the return trip. It is also
suspected that the Chinese have been playing around with
the force of gravity, which has become strangely variable.
Some days it is so heavy that movement is nearly impossible. On other days, it is so slight that all males have
continual erections. But by this time, American society
has become so chaotic that nothing matters to most of
the people except a new religion, The Church of Jesus
Christ the Kidnapped. Its adherents are recognizable by
their rapid and anxious movements as they keep a ner-

vous eye out for the Saviour, who has supposedly returned to earth but has been abducted by unspecified evil
forces.

Wilbur's presidency ends, for all practical purposes,
two-thirds of the way through his second term, and he
dies before he is able to finish his story. *Slapstick* thus
becomes another putdown of utopian schemes, and in
this, as well as in its depiction of a paranoid culture hell-
bent for destruction, it echoes the earlier novels. The
difficulty is that it is too much of an echo. Wilbur's purple
toga reminds one too directly of Bokonon's blue bedspread with the blue tufts. Wilbur's repetition of "Hi ho"
after every ironic turn in the narrative sounds too much
like the "So it goes" of *Slaughterhouse-Five*. And the
miniaturization of the Chinese along with the tidal shifts
in gravity sounds like something Vonnegut would ordi-
narily ascribe to Kilgore Trout. But like all Vonnegut
books, *Slapstick* is wildly funny and disturbing in places,
and it is full of wry comments on American life, comments that enable it to succeed even though it is, to the
longtime reader of Vonnegut, essentially repetitive.

In "The Literature of Exhaustion," John Barth
writes this about the contemporary novelist: "His artistic
victory . . . is that he confronts an intellectual dead end
and employs it against itself to accomplish new human
work."[27] This is certainly what Vonnegut accomplishes
through his cosmic irony as he moves consistently from
his absurdist view of man's meaningless place in the universe and the comic prospects in all human systems and
solutions (such as "Lonesome No More") toward a
paradoxical emphasis on the worth of having some useful
rationalizing fantasy.

"True reality, if it does exist at all," writes one
commentator on Vonnegut's outlook, "can never be
known since it consists of the sum total of all individual
points of view. Given such a Universe, the best man can
do is to try to survive by being pragmatic, by applying a

moral test to help him decide his course of action."[28] Vonnegut comes down to this point in each of his novels, ending up as something of a cosmic moralist as he turns Barth's intellectual dead end (or phrenic asteroid belt) into a type of novel that indeed does blend pop-culture artifacts and contemporary fable into new human work.

3

The "New Reality" of *Slaughterhouse-Five*

"*It is my duty* to describe something beyond the imagination of mankind," the correspondent for the London *Times* began his dispatch in April 1945, after British troops marched into Belsen—the first Nazi prison camp to be exposed to world scrutiny—and discovered over forty thousand malnourished and dying prisoners and more than ten thousand corpses.[1] The problem that Vonnegut faces in all of his novels is essentially the same as the one the correspondent had to face at Belsen—the increasing gap between the horrors of life in the twentieth century and our imaginative ability to comprehend their full actuality.

For Vonnegut, the subject matter is not simply Nazi atrocity; it is many other things—runaway technology, inflated views of human destiny, amoral science, the distribution of wealth in America, the senselessness of war as continued experience, and insanity in Midland City—but the aesthetic problem remains the same, whether the scene is the crystallization of the oceans or the firebombing of Dresden: How to conceptualize and define the night terrors of an era so unreal, so unbelievable, that the very term *fiction* seems no longer to have any currency.

Given the difficulty of the problem that dogs Vonnegut (and most contemporary novelists, for that matter), there is bound to be considerable debate concerning his

success in solving it. The technique he employs in *Player
Piano* offers little in the way of innovation, and Vonnegut
falls considerably short of making a computerized future
seem all that frightening. There are troublesome deficien-
cies in some of his other novels as well—the science-
fiction motifs in *The Sirens of Titan*, as humorously as
they are used, occasionally seem hackneyed; the flat
characterization in *God Bless You, Mr. Rosewater* makes
it difficult to see Eliot Rosewater as much more than a
"tinhorn saint"; and Vonnegut's own appearance at the
Holiday Inn cocktail lounge near the end of *Breakfast of
Champions* is, just about any way one looks at it, a little
contrived.

These are, of course, not major objections to any of
the novels cited, and good arguments could be made for
their artistic merit on other grounds. But there have been
sustained attacks on Vonnegut's writing ever since the
start of his career, doubts that were pretty well summed
up in P. S. Prescott's strident review of *Breakfast of
Champions*. "From time to time, it's nice to have a book
you can hate—it clears the pipes—and I hate this book
for its preciousness, its condescension to its characters,
its self-indulgence, and its facile fatalism: all the lonely
people, their fates sealed in epoxy," Prescott writes.
"Mostly I hate it for its reductiveness, its labored denial
of man's complexity and resilience. Life cannot, as
Vonnegut insists, be summed up with 'and so on' and
'ETC.'—or at least not without more wit and insight than
Vonnegut can master."[2]

Such attacks are not a symptom of vindictiveness
alone. To many critics, Vonnegut's novels do read as if
they are haphazard in structure and simplistic in thought.
Robert Scholes has tried to reply to all this by pointing
out that "Serious critics have shown some reluctance to
acknowledge that Vonnegut is among the great writers of
his generation. He is . . . both too funny and too intelligent for many, who confuse muddled earnestness with

profundity."[3] But the only effective reply is to take a close look at what is probably Vonnegut's most widely read novel and perhaps his best, *Slaughterhouse-Five*.

"I felt after I finished *Slaughterhouse-Five* that I didn't have to write at all anymore if I didn't want to," Vonnegut has said. "It was the end of some sort of career."[4] *Slaughterhouse-Five*, with its non-linear time scheme and its complex interweaving of science-fiction fantasy and the realities of World War II, makes his earlier novels, as innovative as some of them are, appear to be ordinary and uncomplicated by comparison, even if they are far from being that. The reason for this is that Vonnegut reveals himself in *Slaughterhouse-Five*, as do Alexander Trocchi in *Cain's Book* and Thomas Pynchon in *V*, to be "highly self-conscious of the novel as an abstract concept that examines a condition that never yields itself up completely as itself."[5] In other words, the novel functions to reveal new viewpoints in somewhat the same way that the theory of relativity broke through the concepts of absolute space and time. *Slaughterhouse-Five* thus gains its structure from Vonnegut's essential aesthetic problem—how to describe a reality that is beyond human imagination.

The method he chooses is outlined in the explanation given Billy Pilgrim of the Tralfamadorian novel as he is being transported toward that whimsical planet. His captors offer him the only book in English they have, Jacqueline Susann's *Valley of the Dolls*, which is to be placed in a museum. "Billy read it, thought it was pretty good in spots," Vonnegut writes. "The people in it certainly had their ups and downs. But Billy didn't want to read about the same ups and downs over and over again."

The Tralfamadorians allow him to look at some of their novels, but warn that he cannot begin to understand them. The books are small; it would take a dozen of them to even approach *Valley of the Dolls* in bulk, and the language is impossible for Billy. But he can see that the novels consist of clumps of symbols with stars in between. Billy is told that the clumps function something like telegrams, with each clump a message about a situation or scene. But the clumps are not read sequentially as the chapters are in an earthling novel of the ordinary sort. They are read simultaneously. "There isn't any particular relationship between all the messages," the speaker says to Billy, "except that the author has chosen them carefully, so that, when seen all at once, they produce an image of life that is beautiful and surprising and deep. There is no beginning, no middle, no end, no suspense, no moral, no causes, no effects. What we love in our books are the depths of many marvelous moments seen all at one time."

Slaughterhouse-Five is an approximation of this type of novel. Its chapters are divided into short sections (clumps if you will), seldom more than a few paragraphs long. The time-tripping, both by Billy and the narrator, produces an effect somewhat like that achieved in the Tralfamadorian novel—to see many moments at once. The time-tripping also serves to eliminate suspense. (We know not only of Billy's assassination long before the novel ends, but also how the universe will end—the Tralfamadorians blow it up experimenting with a new fuel for their flying saucers.) And the conclusion Vonnegut comes to after examining the causes and effects of Dresden is that there indeed is no moral, only the *Poo-tee-weet* of the bird call that Billy hears when he discovers that the war in Europe is over and he wanders out onto the shady streets of springtime Dresden.

What the Tralfamadorian structure does for Vonnegut is to enable him to embody a new reality in his novel—at least new in contrast to the sequential ups-and-downs reality of the traditional novel. Vonnegut's method accords well with the major changes in the conception of physical reality that have come out of contemporary science. "Change, ambiguity, and subjectivity (in a sense these are synonyms) thus become ways of defining human reality," Jerry H. Bryant writes in commenting on the relationship between twentieth-century physics and recent fiction. "Novelist after novelist examines these features, and expresses almost universal frustration at being deprived of the old stability of metaphysical reality."[6] But not Vonnegut. His Tralfamadorian scheme enables him to overcome the problems of change, ambiguity, and subjectivity involved in objectifying the events surrounding the fire-bombing of Dresden and the involvement of Billy Pilgrim and the author in them.

This is a difficult idea, but one way to understand it is to consider the distinction Bertrand Russell makes in *The ABC of Relativity* between the old view of matter (that it has a definite identity in space and time) and the new view (that it is an event). "An event does not persist and move, like the traditional piece of matter," Russell writes; "it merely exists for a little moment then ceases. A piece of matter will thus be resolved into a series of events. . . . The whole series of these events makes up the whole history of the particle, and the particle is regarded as *being* its history, not some metaphysical entity to which things happen."[7]

This is just the paradoxical conception of Billy that Vonnegut develops. Billy at first seems to be merely an entity to which things happen—he is lost behind the lines during the Battle of the Bulge, he and Roland Weary are captured by the Germans, he survives the fire-bombing of Dresden, he marries, he is the sole survivor of a plane crash, he hallucinates that he is kidnapped by the Tralfamadorians, he appears on crackpot talk-shows, and he is finally gunned down in Chicago. But through the constant movement back and forth in time that constitutes Vonnegut's narrative, we see Billy becoming his history, existing all at once, as if he is an electron. And this gives the novel a structure that is, to directly state the analogy, atomic. Billy whirls around the central fact of Dresden, the planes of his orbits constantly intersecting, and where he has been, he will be.

Of course, all of Vonnegut's earlier central characters are somewhat like Billy in that they are seen as aspects of a protean reality. (Again, the name of Paul Proteus suggests how persistent this representation of personality is.) But it is not until *Slaughterhouse-Five* that Vonnegut develops a way of fully representing the context of that reality. The sudden changes that come over Malachi Constant, Eliot Rosewater, and others make them seem as illusive and problematic as the absurd universe they occupy. By oversimplifying his characters, Vonnegut does manage to suggest something of the complexity of human nature by indirection. But they still tend to linger in the mind as cartoon figures (the Dell paperback covers of *The Sirens of Titan* and *Mother Night* certainly suggest so).

This is not the case with Billy Pilgrim. The Tralfamadorian structure through which his story is told (*sent* might be a better word) gives Billy dimension and substance and brings him eerily to life despite his pale ineffectuality. "Vonnegut's reluctance to depict well-developed characters and to supply them with conventional motives for their actions serves as a conscious burlesque of the whole concept of realism in the novel," Charles B. Harris in his study of the contemporary novel of the absurd has pointed out.[8] But with *Slaughterhouse-Five*, the conscious burlesque is diminished because Vonnegut has come up with a representation of Billy Pilgrim's universe that is in itself a new concept of realism—or reality.

Slaughterhouse-Five is thus as much a novel about writing novels as it is an account of Billy Pilgrim and Dresden. In relating the difficulty he had in dealing with Dresden, Vonnegut prefaces *Slaughterhouse-Five* with an account of his own pilgrimages through time as he tried

to write about his Dresden experience. The opening section consists of jumps back and forth in the author's
life—from his return to Dresden on a Guggenheim grant
to his return home from the war two decades earlier,
from a conversation on the telephone with his old war
buddy to the end of the war in a beet field on the Elbe
outside of Halle, and then on to the Chicago City News
Bureau, Schenectady and General Electric, visiting O'Hare
in Pennsylvania, teaching writing at the University of
Iowa, and then Dresden and the Guggenheim trip once
more.

The concern is always with the problem of writing
the book—how to represent imaginatively things that are
unimaginable—but in detailing his frustrations, Vonnegut
conceptualizes his own life the way he later does Billy's,
in terms of Tralfamadorian time theory. The structure of
the chapter about writing the novel consequently prefig-
ures the structure of the novel itself.

In that opening section, Vonnegut outlines his essential difficulty by elaborating on the misconception with
which he began work on the novel. He states that he
thought the book would be easy to write—all he would
have to do is to simply report what he had seen. But this
does not work. Too many other things get in the way.
Why was Dresden, a supposedly safe city, bombed? Why
did the American and British governments cover up the
facts about the raid? What does the Dresden attack imply
about American and British civilization? And, more important, why must Vonnegut's life always lead up to and
go back to what he saw when he emerged from the
slaughterhouse meat locker and looked at the moonscape
that was once perhaps the most beautiful city in Europe?

The conflict Vonnegut is indicating is that of the old
Henry James–H. G. Wells debate on what the novel as a
literary form should be. James felt that it should be
mimetic, realistic, that it should relate human experience
as accurately as possible through detailed characteriza-

tion and careful construction. Wells, on the other hand, believed that social pronouncements and ideas are more important, and that art should be subordinate to both. Wells was not even certain that the novel should be taken seriously as an art form. For him, characterization was just something to be got through so that an idea or a "ventilation" of the novel's social, political, or philosophical point can be got across as clearly as possible.[9]

Wells's influence is certainly a factor in the development of the science-fiction novel, and James must be taken into account in any discussion of the so-called mainstream or art novel. Vonnegut, as he indicates in his preface to *Slaughterhouse-Five*, is caught somewhere in the middle of the debate. His earlier books are mainly novels of character written to a thesis, an approach that leads to the direct statement of a moral in *Mother Night*.

But *Slaughterhouse-Five* is different; Vonnegut's impulse is to begin with his own experience, not with characters or ideas, but the ideas soon get in the way.

Two structural possibilities come to mind. The first is suggested in the song Vonnegut remembers as he thinks about how useless, yet how obsessive, the Dresden part of his memory has been:

> My name is Yon Yonson,
> I work in Wisconsin,
> I work in a lumbermill there,
> The people I meet when I walk down the street,
> They say, "What's your name?"
> And I say,
> "My name is Yon Yonson,
> I work in Wisconsin. . . ."

When people ask him what *he* is working on, Vonnegut says that for years he has been telling them the same thing—a book about Dresden. Like Yon Yonson, he seems doomed to repeat the answer endlessly. But the maddening song suggests something else—the tendency many people (perhaps all) have to return to a central point in their lives in reply to the question of identity ("What's your name?").

The song also crudely suggests the time theory that is later developed in the novel with its emphasis on infinite repetition. But repetition leads nowhere, especially in a novel, so Vonnegut considers another possibility. He takes a roll of wallpaper, and on the back of it tries to make an outline of the story using his daughter's crayons (a different color for each of the characters). "And the blue line met the red line and then the yellow line," Vonnegut writes, "and the yellow line stopped because the character represented by the yellow line was dead. And so on. The destruction of Dresden was represented by a vertical band of orange cross-hatching, and all the lines that were still alive passed through it, came out the other side." This is an outline for a Jamesian novel with an essentially linear time scheme. But it does not work as a representation of the experience Vonnegut is anxious to write about.

For one thing, characters do not actually come out the other side and inevitably go on from there. Like Vonnegut himself, like Yon Yonson, they compulsively return, moving back and forth on their lines. And as for the lines that stop, the beginning and middle of those lines are still there. What does Vonnegut do? He comes up with a structure that includes both the Yon Yonson story and the wallpaper outline. It is as if he rolls the wallpaper into a tube so all of the characters and incidents are closely layered, so they are in effect one unit, and the reader must look at them from the side. The tube then becomes a telescope through which the reader looks into the fourth dimension, or at least into another dimension of the novel. The story goes around and around, yet it still leads somewhere, and yet the end is very close to the beginning.

It may well be that, as Karen and Charles Wood

suggest, *Slaughterhouse-Five* is a new form of novel representing the mature fusion of science fiction and Jamesian literature of experience.[10]

The search for an approach also takes Vonnegut
through an investigation of other works of literature that
deal with catastrophe and the attitudes that surround it.
He mentions an account of the Children's Crusade in a
nineteenth-century book, *Extraordinary Popular Delusions and the Madness of Crowds*. This account is used
to underscore the contrast he draws between the serious
business of war and the naiveté of Billy Pilgrim, Roland
Weary, and most of the other soldiers he depicts. He
mentions *Dresden, History, Stage and Gallery*, by Mary
Endell (published 1908), and its account of how Dresden, with all of its beauty, has been attacked repeatedly.

He quotes some lines from Theodore Roethke's
Words for the Wind to suggest both his own confusion
and the sense he has that, simply by moving ahead and
back in time, the meaning of Dresden was being sorted
out:

> I wake to sleep, and take my waking slow.
> I feel my fate in what I cannot fear.
> I learn by going where I have to go.

He mentions Erica Ostrovsky's *Céline and His Vision* and recounts how death and time also obsessed the
insomniac French writer after he was wounded in World
War I. And then he mentions the story of the destruction
of Sodom and Gomorrah in the Bible and how Lot's wife,
because of her compulsive looking back at the burning
cities when she was told not to, was turned into a pillar of
salt.

All of these references either give Vonnegut ideas
and material or else they relate to his own reaction to
Dresden, but they do not quite offer him the approach he
is after. This, as we have seen, he had to discover for
himself.

The structure Vonnegut chooses is indicated right at the start of Billy Pilgrim's story. It is a structure that, for all of the later explanation and illustration of its basis in Tralfamadorian time theory, actually develops out of Vonnegut's central character. Vonnegut, in the guise of an oral storyteller, asks us to "Listen." Then, in two paragraphs he introduces Billy and sets up the pattern that will be followed throughout the rest of the novel: "Billy Pilgrim has come unstuck in time. . . . He has seen his birth and death many times, he says, and pays random visits to all the events in between."

Vonnegut proceeds to outline Billy's life in the next few pages—what happens to him during the war, his marriage, the airplane crash, the flying saucer, and his appearances on talk shows—to build irony and to bring out the sudden and often absurdly sad changes in Billy's life that make his time-tripping largely a survival reaction.

Billy's survival seems at first to depend simply on his thinness as a character, his ineffectuality, and his utter insignificance. But the imagery associated with Billy, as it expands and cuts back and forth through the novel, suggests otherwise. He is said at times to look like a Coke bottle in shape and like a filthy flamingo in dress, and he is said to have a "chest and shoulders like a box of kitchen matches." But before his capture by the Germans he is portrayed "like a poet in the Parthenon." When he is elected president of the Ilium Lions Club in 1957, he gets up to give his acceptance speech in a voice that is a "gorgeous instrument." He becomes as "rich as Croesus." At another point in his travels through time, he is clearly identified with Christ, "self-crucified, holding himself there with a blue and ivory claw hooked over the sill of the ventilator." Billy is anything but a thin character; he is another illustration of Vonnegut's concept of Protean man. Billy *needs* to travel back and forth in time not only to understand himself but also to endure himself, to be-

come his history. He is many personalities, many selves
existing together at once. He is a living Tralfamadorian
"clump."

One of the surprises in the novel is that the personality that seems the most ridiculous—Billy as an optometrist—turns out to be the most important symbolically. Throughout the novel there is considerable
emphasis on seeing things, and there is a near continuous
contrast between the way the world looks to Billy and the
way others see him. At times Billy appears to be a poet
and at other times, such as when he appears in Dresden
wrapped in an azure curtain and wearing silver-painted
combat boots, he looks the fool. For Billy himself, there
is considerable development in the way he views what has
happened to him.

The change that comes over Billy is mainly a result
of the way he is forced to look at many things—Weary's
triangular-bladed knife with its brass-knuckle grip, the
picture of a woman attempting sexual intercourse with a
Shetland pony, the German corporal's boots (in which
Billy sees a vision of Adam and Eve), his Cadillac El
Dorado Coupe de Ville in the suburban shopping center
parking lot outside his office, the spastic salesman who
comes to the door trying to peddle phony magazine sub-
scriptions, St. Elmo's fire around the heads of the guards
and his fellow prisoners, the cozy interior of the guards'
railroad car, the clock on his gas stove an hour before the
flying saucer comes to pick him up, the backward movie
he watches on television while he is waiting for the
Tralfamadorians, and so on. Through recapitulating
imagery, Vonnegut suggests how the simultaneous relationship of everything Billy sees and experiences is slowly
revealed and how Tralfamadorian time theory, instead of
merely being a comic example of Vonnegut's fondness
for science-fiction motifs, develops naturally and logically
out of Billy's unconscious awareness of his own life.

Vonnegut's use of recapitulating imagery can be

seen on almost every page of the novel, but the backward
movie will serve as one of the best examples of this technique. Billy suddenly sees a movie of World War II run-
ning backward in his head. The bombers suck the fire and
the bombs back into their bellies, the bombs are shipped
back to the factories and dismantled, and the dangerous
contents are reduced to mineral form and returned to the
ground. The fliers turn in their uniforms and become high-
school kids. Hitler and everyone else turns into a baby
and, as Vonnegut writes, "all humanity, without excep-
tion, conspired biologically to produce two perfect people
named Adam and Eve. . . ." The reference to Adam and
Eve recapitulates the vision Billy saw in the German corporal's boot years before; and the barking of the dog he
hears outside his house recapitulates the barking Billy
heard just before the corporal captured him.

A further use of this type of imagery occurs when
Billy hears what he thinks is the cry of a melodious owl,
but the sound turns out to be the whine of the flying
saucer. All his professional life he has been working with
an "owl" of another sort. During one of his time trips,
Billy opens his eyes and finds himself "staring into the
glass eyes of a jade green mechanical owl. The owl was
hanging upside down from a rod of stainless steel. The
owl was Billy's optometer in his office in Ilium. An
optometer is an instrument for measuring refractive errors in eyes—in order that corrective lenses may be prescribed." With this recapitulation of imagery, a major
theme in the novel is brought into focus.

Of all that Billy is forced to look at, the most significant is what is revealed to him by the Tralfamadorians.
The flying saucer becomes an optometer that measures
the refractive errors in Billy's outlook and the Tralfamadorians are able to suggest a prescription. But it is
Billy's job as an optometrist to help others see, and this is
what he tries to do. At first, he is not very effective. He is
able to attend the Ilium School of Optometry for only

one semester before he is drafted (and he is enrolled only in *night* sessions at that). And after the war, despite all his success, Billy is dealing less in vision than in fashion: "Frames are where the money is." But through his flying-saucer journey, he gains a new conception of what his job should be—prescribing "corrective lenses for Earthling souls" so that they can see into the fourth dimension as the Tralfamadorians do.

This development of Billy's vision is handled in a deceptively ambiguous way, of course. The repetition of imagery together with the juxtaposition of disparate events in Billy's life suggests that his trip to Tralfamadore is an hallucination and that the prescription he winds up advocating is essentially the result of the associative powers of his mind. The substance of his trip to Tralfamadore may well be the consequence of reading a Kilgore Trout novel, and the whole business of time travel and the simultaneous existence of events may well be simply another of the human illusions Vonnegut attacks so frequently in his earlier novels.

But the point for Billy is that the Tralfamadorians *are* real, that the years of his life are the only time there is, and he is going to live every moment over and over again. In addition, there is the pragmatic value of his vision—it enables him to deal with the horror of Dresden and to get around the question of "Why me?" that echoes through the novel. Are his lenses rose-colored or not? It perhaps depends on the reader's own willingness to look into the fourth dimension with him. *Slaughterhouse-Five*, at any rate, gives us a glimpse of what that dimension might be like, and shows us at the very least how it is possible to gain a sense of purpose in life by doing what Billy Pilgrim does—he re-invents himself and his universe.

The process of re-invention is made vivid by Vonnegut's style with its hesitant short sentences and his tendency to return again and again to the same images.

His abruptness works well in describing the time shifts
Billy suddenly goes through, and it contributes a sense of
Billy's new vision, his re-invented universe, being formu-
lated piece by piece. But the overall effect of the direct,
often choppy, sentences and the brief paragraphs (several
times consisting of only a few words) is to suggest the
whirring of basic particles, of electrons that really cannot
be seen. What we think of when we think of the structure
of the atom is not actually there at all—it is only a
model, an illusion. And the same thing can be said of
Slaughterhouse-Five and Billy Pilgrim's erratic revolu-
tions in time around Dresden. But as a model, it is,
through its recapitulating imagery, its optometric symbol-
ism, its positively charged sentences, and its telegraphic-
Tralfamadorian-atomic structure, one of the best solutions
we have to the problem of describing the unimaginable.

Unfortunately, one cannot say the same of the
movie version of the novel released in 1972. Although
Michael Sacks as Billy Pilgrim and Valerie Perrine as
Montana Wildhack are effective and director George Roy
Hill (who also directed *Butch Cassidy and the Sundance
Kid*) and writer Stephen Geller treat the story with rever-
ence, the film does not match the sophistication of statement to be found in the book. One problem is that while
Billy's time-tripping is handled in an artistically justifying
way by Vonnegut, it is merely cinematically familiar on
the screen where flashbacks and flash-forwards only serve
to diminish its intellectual force.

There are many nice touches in the film, however.
One is Billy's changing into Nazi-looking steel-rimmed
glasses in middle age (a device that hints at the recapitulating imagery in the novel). And there are some bril-
liantly conceived scenes, such as one of American soldiers
marching through Dresden, past the spires and statues of
the city, while the Fourth Brandenburg Concerto comes
over the soundtrack. Much of the film was shot in Prague
by Miroslav Ondricek, the Czech photographer who did

Forman's *Loves of a Blonde* and Ivan Passer's *Intimate Lightning*, and Ondricek deserves much of the credit for the visually pleasing aspects of the production. But, as one reviewer wrote, "In its elaborate structure and editing, its leaping bounds between fact and fancy, the film is like a version of *Last Year in Marienbad* revised for showing on *Sesame Street*."[11]

Of course, no film could document the way Vonnegut confronted his own ambiguous nature in working out the story of Billy Pilgrim. The character who is developed the most fully in the novel is Vonnegut himself.[12] This is why Vonnegut can get away with repeating the phrase, "So it goes," after every tragic or pathetic incident. He has established himself, through his preface, as one of the characters in the book. His is a human voice, not just that of an omniscient narrator, and this in itself adds poignancy to the inhuman acts his subject matter forces him to describe.

Vonnegut's way of dealing with that subject matter results in a novel that is, by any standard, highly complex. It is a novel that works toward the resolution of Vonnegut's own obsessions at the same time it works toward the resolution of several nervous questions concerning the viability of the genre itself. Like many of his contemporaries, Vonnegut accepts the idea of an absurd universe that is chaotic and without meaning. But unlike Beckett and Robbe-Grillet, he does not develop an anti-style, even though he seems to share their fear of the loss of distinctions between fact and fiction. Instead, he chooses to rely upon many traditional devices (among them burlesque and parody) in conjunction with the new reality of twentieth-century physics and the motifs of science fiction to come up with a radical use of fictional form that reveals a regained joy in storytelling and is also true to his cosmically ironic vision.

4

Science Fiction

One thing that is certainly apparent in a survey of Vonnegut's novels is that he refuses to limit himself to a single mode of fiction. Each of his novels is, in fact, an example of modal multiplicity. At times he combines techniques drawn from the novel of manners, from the confessional novel, and from the detective novel, as well as drawing on devices from soap operas and the slick magazine stories of the 1950s. But one form of fiction is drawn upon more consistently and more fascinatingly than any of the others, and that, of course, is science fiction, which is so apparent in his writing that it is the label he has been stuck with ever since *Player Piano*.

Vonnegut is not comfortable with this classification and has complained that he has been "a soreheaded occupant of a file drawer labeled 'science fiction'" for too long and that he would like out because "many serious critics regularly mistake the drawer for a urinal."[1] Some aficianados of science fiction are no more comfortable than Vonnegut is with his sf reputation. Brian W. Aldiss, for instance, in *Billion Year Spree: The True History of Science Fiction*, states that "Kurt Vonnegut has not improved since he has been voted one of America's heap big gurus" and that "Vonnegut sped right out of the science-fiction field as soon as he had cash for the gasoline."[2] Vonnegut may not be a science-fiction writer in the strictest sense, but he most certainly uses the motifs of that form as metaphors of his own humorous vision, finding in the conventions of science fiction "not a kind of restriction but a way of releasing his own sentimental-ironic view of a meaningless universe redeemed by love."[3]

Time travel, visits by creatures from other planets, flying saucers, glimpses into a nightmare future—these and other science-fiction motifs are employed by Vonnegut to make the reader more aware of the absurdity of man's place in the universe. Vonnegut uses science fiction as a means of transmitting his vision, a vision that, because of its cosmically ironic implications, demands the intergalactic scope that science fiction affords. Given Vonnegut's attitudes toward his characters, if there were no such form as science fiction, he would be forced to invent it.

"But if the science-fiction metaphor offers Vonnegut his greatest freedom in demonstrating his negative vision," G. K. Wolfe writes in *The Journal of Popular Culture*, "it also offers the reader the greatest anesthetic against this vision. In a context of fantasy, the idea of haphazard forces governing human life seems less frightening than when grounded in an identifiable historical context. . . ."[4] Science fiction thus also serves as a mitigating element in Vonnegut's fiction as well as a means of carrying off many of the jokes that run through and structure his novels.

Vonnegut himself has emphasized the humorous purpose of science fiction in his writing, pointing out that "the science-fiction passages in *Slaughterhouse-Five* are just like the clowns in Shakespeare: . . . trips to other planets, science fiction of an obviously kidding sort, is equivalent to bringing on the clowns every so often to lighten things up."[5] Vonnegut accordingly uses science fiction not only as a way of carrying his ideas but as a

way of making those ideas more palatable. If it were not
for the science-fiction elements, Vonnegut would often be
very unfunny indeed.

But the extent to which Vonnegut actually is a
science-fiction writer is a question that can easily be given
more emphasis than it perhaps deserves, because science
fiction is as much a publisher's marketing category as it is
a literary genre. It is partly this that Vonnegut objects to
in the categorization he has received—that he has been
the victim of what is in effect simply a packaging definition. But science fiction as a type of writing has a tradition of its own and, more important, it represents an
approach to a definition of man and his status in the
universe that accords nicely with Vonnegut's own attitudes.

Science fiction is in a major sense a reaction against
realism or the "single reality" fiction of the nineteenth
century, when the Victorian notion that the universe
could be comprehended in terms of easily understood
formulas and that life was earnest and real was generally
accepted. "Today, after Einstein, Freud, psychedelics,
quantum mechanics, McLuhan, cybernetics, the Heisen-
berg Uncertainty Principle, systems analysis, and a few
other little vision-expanders, we're back where we were
before the Victorians defined reality as a rigid Tinker Toy
construct," Norman Spinrad writes in the introduction to
his anthology, *Modern Science Fiction.* "We know that a
literature which pretends that it is somehow more relevant to the 'real world' . . . because it deals with the 'here-
and-now' is putting itself on. There is no fixed 'here' and
no fixed 'now,' only the continuous kaleidoscopic explo-
sion of the evolving human mind in a total space-time
universe that is itself revolving new realities around us
faster than we can catch our breath."[6] This is just the
point implied by Vonnegut's cosmic irony with its continuous laughter at systems and philosophies and its

paradoxically pragmatic attempts at dealing with the new view of reality.

Despite the congruity of the science-fiction approach for Vonnegut, he plays down its influence on him. Unlike a lot of other science-fiction writers, Vonnegut states that he did not get into reading and trading the old science-fiction pulp magazines as a boy. Instead, he read only a few of the older fantasists, such as H. G. Wells or Robert Louis Stevenson. He was attracted to the form when he was working for General Electric after the war and saw a computer-operated milling machine. "*Player Piano* was my response to the implication of having everything run by little boxes," he has said. "The idea of doing that, you know, made sense, perfect sense. To have a little clicking box make all the decisions wasn't a vicious thing to do. But it was too bad for human beings who get their dignity from their jobs."[7] So he "cheerfully ripped off the plot of *Brave New World*," worked out the woeful implications of computerization, thought up some new gadgets, and wrote a futuristic novel that contains a central science-fiction theme—fascination with the way technology changes the social environment—and got Vonnegut, for better or for worse, a lifelong membership in the club.

However much Vonnegut discounts the influence of science fiction on his early development, its evolution as a literary form has much to do with his popularity and it seems to have acted as the inspiration for several of his novels. The immediate history of science fiction begins with Hugo Gernsback who founded *Amazing Stories* magazine in 1926. Gernsback had the notion of "scientifiction" as a way of educating the masses in science. (He tried the same idea on a different subject later in another publication, *Sexology*.) The problem with the stories Gernsback obtained is one that would serve for years to stereotype science fiction—most of the stories turned out to be formula pieces written by hacks for a penny a word. But *Amazing Stories* caught on, partly

because the fixed-reality fiction published in other magazines of the 1920s was out of touch with the times. As
bad as the fiction in *Amazing Stories* was, it at least took
into account and emphasized the importance of technological development on the modern frame of mind. "The
literary critics of the day had no term for this mind-
blowing, consciousness-expanding literary effect," Spinrad writes, "but the early science-fiction fans had a good
one. They called it 'Sense of Wonder.' "[8]

Fandom started early, and soon after *Amazing
Stories* came out, a subculture emerged. From the first,
science fiction has been associated with an underground,
with a select minority who can read, appreciate, and dis-
cuss its often weird implications. The birth of this subculture anticipated much of what happened during the
1960s when devotees congregated around gurus or rock
musicians or even such writers as Robert A. Heinlein and
Vonnegut himself, both of whose work seemed to embody the most appealing of all science-fiction characteris-
tics, the mating of magic and science.

The underground appeal of science fiction has long
been strengthened by the often bizarre and mysterious
qualities of the writers themselves. An important figure in
this respect was John W. Campbell, Jr., who edited and
wrote for *Astounding Science Fiction* and its successor
Analog from 1937 until his death in 1971. Unlike Gernsback, Campbell insisted on valid science in the stories he
accepted for publication. Trained as an engineer, Campbell demanded scientific credibility from his writers and
consequently became the single most influential editor in
the development of science fiction as a literary form. But
he was a fantastic figure. He championed many outland-
ish causes, including ESP, antigravity devices, dowsing,
and astrological weather forecasts. Campbell seemed to
see himself as a "scientific visionary, the lone hero ad-
vancing the cause of man's understanding and mastery of

the universe through inspired personal effort: Faust as an existential hero in a reality without a Mephistopheles."[9]

An intriguing question as far as Vonnegut's relationship to Campbell is concerned involves the name Vonnegut chose for the central character of *Mother Night*, Howard W. Campbell, Jr. Whether by this Vonnegut intended merely a jest at John W. Campbell, Jr.'s expense, Aldiss asks, "or whether he implied a profound commentary on Campbell as the greatest purveyor of pulp power fantasy, I must leave wiser critics to decide."[10]

The similarity in names suggests, however, that Vonnegut did have something in mind. Perhaps it is the moral of *Mother Night*, that we are what we pretend to be, so it is important that we be careful about what we choose to pretend. John W. Campbell, Jr., apparently had some difficulty determining where pretending started and where it ended as far as the science in science fiction is concerned. He began to devote space in his magazines to pushing such dubious discoveries as the Dean Drive, which was supposed to produce thrust while miraculously avoiding generating an equal and opposite reaction. In some ways John W. Campbell, Jr., seemed to practice something like the sort of willful self-delusion Vonnegut's Howard is given over to.

But despite his eccentricities (perhaps because of them) Campbell attracted a number of important writers to his publications in the 1940s. There was A. E. Van Vogt, who in the novel *Slan* combined ESP with the idea of the Nietzschean superman and came out with the human mutant as a successor to man. (This, of course, introduced what has since developed into something of a science-fiction archetype.) Robert A. Heinlein, a former naval officer, had poor style and characterization, but Campbell appreciated his ability to visualize future worlds. Heinlein later became famous for *Stranger in a Strange Land*, which, with its messianic hero, developed a considerable cult following in the 1960s. (Charles

Manson was one of many who thought he detected secret messages in *Stranger*.) Isaac Asimov, with a Ph.D. in chemistry, more perfectly fit Campbell's conception of the scientifically informed writer. (Asimov actually supported himself writing science fiction while getting his degree.) Asimov wrote a long series of stories and novels on robots (*I, Robot*) as well as *The Foundation Trilogy*, which deals with the Spenglerian rise, decline, and rebirth of a galactic empire. But the strangest of Campbell's proteges is L. Ron Hubbard.

Hubbard, who thought himself a facsimile of the Van Vogtian superman and the Heinlein messiah combined, stood up at a convention of science-fiction writers in 1949 and, in what seemed at the time to merely be a jocular speech, said, "Writing for a penny a word is ridiculous. If a man really wanted to make a million dollars, the best way would be to start his own religion."[11]

The next year Hubbard demonstrated that he was serious, publishing *Dianetics: The Modern Science of Mental Health* and founding the religion that is now known as Scientology. At first Hubbard simply advocated a form of counseling known as "auditing," which involved the eradication of "engrams," or negative memories. Once freed of engrams, a convert was known as a "Clear." But through a combination of Hinduism and Buddhism, Hubbard later claimed to have discovered the real nature of the human soul, or "Thetan," which he maintains is reincarnated thousands of times.

Scientology now claims at least four-million followers worldwide, and Hubbard has enjoyed the comforts of a 3,300-ton yacht, which has also been used as a seagoing schoolhouse for courses in Scientology. (It costs $625 for "Life Repair," $5,000 to reach "Clear," and considerably more to reach "Operating Thetan," the rank of Hubbard himself.) In addition, Scientologists have paid cash in recent years for properties in New York,

Boston, Washington, D. C., Miami, St. Louis, Los Angeles, and San Diego. Although Campbell most likely did not anticipate expansion of this sort, he did champion Scientology in the pages of *Astounding Science Fiction.*

Hubbard's influence on Vonnegut seems to be more than a little apparent. In addition to the resemblance between Eliot Rosewater and Hubbard (Eliot also winds up taking himself seriously as a messianic figure), there is the matter of Hubbard's advice about founding a religion. His turned out to be Scientology; Vonnegut's turned out to be Bokononism. And just as Scientology got Hubbard off the penny-a-word treadmill, Bokononism, via *Cat's Cradle,* gave Vonnegut the cult following that led to his popular (and financial) success in the 1960s.

The cultishness surrounding the development of science fiction and its importance to the success of certain science-fiction writers is something that needs emphasis. As Spinrad explains, by the end of the 1940s, science-fiction writers were "feeding back murky adolescent longings for power, strength, peer-group solidarity, and mystic transcendence, and by so doing were drawing together tribal cults around their works, creating pocket universes of which they were the little gods and thereby altering reality itself."[12] Fan magazines were started, thousands of science-fiction readers nationwide adopted the motto "Fans Are Slans" in reference to the Van Vogt novel, and world science-fiction conventions were held.

The influence of Campbell, the growth of a subculture, the growing awareness of the new world brought on by technology, and the general improvement in the quality of science-fiction writing led to a science-fiction boom, and an inevitable bust. New magazines were founded almost daily. Some, such as *Galaxy* and the *Magazine of Fantasy and Science Fiction,* published much excellent work. But by the mid-1950s, more than forty magazines were on the market and much bad writing was the result. Meaningful work was buried in the avalanche and cheap packaging led to a negative image as it became increasingly difficult for readers and reviewers to sort the best work out. Some writers quit in disgust. Others, such as Theodore Sturgeon, Philip Jose Farmer, and Philip K. Dick hung on, sometimes at considerable personal and economic cost, their predicaments somewhat suggestive of the enduring plight of Vonnegut's Kilgore Trout.

Too much stylization led to another difficulty. "The trouble with genre material is that it becomes overused," Aldiss comments. "On the whole, the props are few: rocket ships, telepathy, robots, time-travel, other dimensions, huge machines, aliens, future wars."[13] It soon became impossible to use the props seriously without inviting self-parody; and Vonnegut certainly realized this when he discovered that they worked very well as subservient vehicles for his cosmic irony and existential wit.

The bursting of the science-fiction bubble in the 1950s led to a revolution in the genre in the 1960s that, of course, coincided with Vonnegut's success. The revolution involved a number of younger writers, a "new wave," composed in part by Thomas M. Disch, James Sallis, and Spinrad, all of whom had grown up within the altered context of "the multivalued post-Age of Reason."[14] To these writers, the older single-reality fiction with its linear conception of time simply did not accord with their generational consciousness.

In addition, there was a drift toward environmental topics, providing a theme that, because of its urgency, seemed dramatically new—technology's debasement of man and his surroundings. *Cat's Cradle* is the most memorable book to come out of this drift, but it was accompanied by a whole spate of catastrophe novels involving not *ice-nine* but snow (John Boland's *White August*), gales (J. G. Ballard's *The Wind from Nowhere*), plague (John Blackburn's *The Scent of New-Mown Hay*), and vanishing oceans (Charles Eric Maine's *The Tides Went Out*).

Vonnegut's development parallels the development of science fiction in the last forty years in many ways. Not only does he draw from the form, but he appears to have been aware of its intimate changes and was influenced by the work and ideas of such figures as John W. Campbell, Jr., and Hubbard, as well as by other, less bizarre figures such as Arthur C. Clarke and Asimov. Vonnegut turns and twists these influences for humorous reasons that often are obscure, but the influences are there nonetheless.

But, as even his first novel demonstrates, Vonnegut refuses to be limited by either the form of science fiction or its conventions. He shows from the start in *Player Piano* that he differs from most science-fiction writers in his characterization. Even though Vonnegut tends toward cartoonlike characters in his novels, purposely avoiding full development on principle, he nonetheless begins with a character, Paul Proteus, rather than an idea. Science may provide the conflict, but the resolution comes through character.

Most of Vonnegut's fiction concerns itself with technological problems but only insofar as those problems relate to and explicate character, with the point usually being that no matter what technology surrounds them, men and women remain essentially the same.[15] *Player Piano* despite its EPICAC XIV computer and its checker-playing machine, comes down in the end to an ironic story about a disappointed middle-class revolutionist, however much it echoes and anticipates other novels, such as B. F. Skinner's *Walden II* and Ray Bradbury's *Fahrenheit 451*, that deal with man's performance in an authoritarian society.

Like these novels, *Player Piano* depicts a questionable future for the human race and does it in a way that is hardly original. As Vonnegut has indicated, he stole the plot from *Brave New World*, and he could have picked up the idea of a machine-dominated society from any number of sources. One of these is the story, "Twilight," by John W. Campbell, Jr., in which a time traveler narrates an account of an era when man has abandoned whole cities to machines, yet the machines drone on endlessly, serving masters who are no longer there. None of this is what makes *Player Piano* at all memorable, however; it is the characterization of Paul Proteus that brings it to life.

Vonnegut relies more heavily on science-fiction motifs in *The Sirens of Titan*, but it too depends more on the sufferings and delusions of Malachi Constant and Winston Niles Rumfoord than it does on the trappings of space travel, time warps, strange life forms, robots, and anti-utopia. Nonetheless, Vonnegut makes more use of these sf standbys in *The Sirens of Titan* than in any other novel. The result is "a cascade of absurd invention, its hither-thither technique a sophisticated pinch from the Wide Screen Baroque school. The elaboration of plot makes it read like an exceptionally funny Dick novel."[16] Dick is a science-fiction writer (*The Martian Time-Slip* and *The Penultimate Truth*) who uses the form much like Vonnegut does. That is, he is as much a member of the school of Pirandello as he is of Campbell in emphasizing that things are never what they seem. His work is full of scarecrow people, robots bothered by conscience, and hallucinations and illusion on almost every page—a description that also corresponds, point by point, to that of *The Sirens of Titan*, a novel that certainly is not as unusual a work of science fiction as some readers have assumed, even though its humor is matchless in the field.

Vonnegut's comic use of the chrono-synclastic infundibulum and the spastic wanderings of Rumfoord and Kazak, the hound of space, in *The Sirens of Titan*, comes in for considerable satire in a parody of the Vonnegut style and imagination in the recently published *Venus of the Half-Shell*, purportedly by Kilgore Trout (but actually by Philip Jose Farmer).

In *Venus on the Half-Shell*, Simon Wagstaff, the Space Wanderer, wearing a black eyepatch over his left eye and always carrying an atomic-powered electrical banjo, roams the cosmos in a Chinese spaceship, a dog, an owl, and a female robot his constant companions, hoping to find an answer to the question that torments him every moment of his picaresque existence—Why are we created only to suffer and die? The parody is wildly funny as it takes Simon to the equal-time planet, the *No Smoking* planet, and the prison planet, among others. In the course of his travels, he experiences a variety of extraterrestrial sexual customs, and is fitted with a prehensile tail on the planet Dokal.

Simon finally reaches the world of the Clerun-Gowph, where, while drinking beer with Bingo, the wisest man on the planet, he learns that the universe was created as a scientific experiment by a power that went out for lunch one day and forgot to come back. Simon asks why such an experiment would ever have been started when anyone could foresee that it would cause sextillions of living beings to suffer for nothing. Old Bingo pours a beer down, belches, and muses, "Why not?"[17]

In addition to being a satiric commentary on *The Sirens of Titan*, *Venus on the Half-Shell* points to one of Vonnegut's most effectively used science-fiction motifs—his inclusion of Kilgore Trout novels in *God Bless You, Mr. Rosewater*, *Slaughterhouse-Five*, and *Breakfast of Champions*. Since the Trout novels almost always deal with life on another planet or the mishaps of alien creatures when they arrive on earth, the books serve to increase the cosmic irony that Vonnegut relies upon so much. "Trout's favorite formula was to describe a perfectly hideous society, not unlike his own," Vonnegut writes in introducing his alter ego in *Rosewater*, "and then toward the end, to suggest ways in which it can be improved."

It is a Trout novel, *2BR02B*, that posits the problem that serves to motivate Eliot Rosewater, "What in hell are people for?" And it is a Trout novel, *The Gospel from Outer Space*, with its ironic retelling of the Christian message that indicates the sort of Christ figure Billy Pilgrim becomes in *Slaughterhouse-Five*. But it is in *Breakfast of Champions* that Vonnegut makes the most extensive use of Trout's 117 novels. (Trout is also reputed to have written several thousand short stories.)

The Trout novels retold in *Breakfast of Champions* are remarkably similar to Vonnegut's own in their resolutions and in their tendency to avoid any actual technical explanation of the strange futuristic technologies they rely upon. A good example is the story of Delmore Skag, who, as a way of protesting against the wastefulness and absurdity of large families, invents a means of reproducing replicas of himself by shaving living cells from the palm of his right hand and culturing them in chicken soup. He then invites his neighbors, all of whom have large families, to mass baptisms—sometimes as many as a hundred of his "babies" at once. But instead of passing a law outlawing families of more than one or two children, the government enacts legislation prohibiting the possession of chicken soup by an unmarried person. And the cosmically ironic joke is on Delmore Skag, a joke that goes along with one of Vonnegut's main themes—the destruction of the planet through the insane response human beings seem to make to any idea.

Another example of this type of story is that of Kago and his brave little homosexual crew (all only an inch high) from the planet Zeltoldimar, who carry the secret of the automobile to earth. They do not know, as Vonnegut writes, "that human beings could be as easily felled by a single idea as by cholera or the bubonic plague. There was no immunity to cuckoo ideas on Earth." Less than a century after Kago's arrival, automobiles were killing everything on earth. Kago is so disturbed by what he has done that, in desperation, he goes

to a bar in Detroit and tries to lecture on the evils of the
internal-combustion engine. A drunken automobile
worker mistakes him for a match and kills him by trying
to strike him on the underside of the bar.

In one novel, *Cat's Cradle*, however, Vonnegut
plays things straighter, especially with the substance that
engenders the final catastrophe—*ice-nine*. Vonnegut generally makes no attempt to explain or make plausible the
scientific wonders that occur in his futuristic worlds, and
there admittedly is not much "science" in his fiction. But
with *ice-nine*, at any rate, Vonnegut provides a technical
lecture that makes *Cat's Cradle* read at times more like
hard-core science fiction than any of Vonnegut's other
novels. This lecture occurs when Dr. Breed of the same
research laboratory at which Dr. Hoenikker worked tells
Jonah that "There are several ways in which certain
liquids can crystallize—can freeze—several ways in
which their atoms can stack in an orderly, rigid way." Dr.
Breed goes on to talk about crystals of ethylene diamine
tartrate and seeds of undesired crystal patterns. The result is a suggestion of authentic science that makes the
apocalyptic ending of the novel horrifying, despite
Vonnegut's comic implications.

There are, by the way, several interesting side notes
on *ice-nine* and *Cat's Cradle*. Vonnegut says he got the
idea through an account he heard of H. G. Wells's visit to
the General Electric laboratory in Schenectady. General
Electric officials told Irving Langmuir, the Nobel Prize
winner, to think up something that would entertain Wells,
so Langmuir made up a story about a form of ice that
stayed crystallized at room temperature. He thought that
Wells might want to use the concept himself. Wells was
not very impressed; but Vonnegut obviously was. A few
years later, Vonnegut asked a crystallographer at a cocktail party whether *ice-nine* could be, at least theoretically,
possible. "He put his cocktail glass on the mantelpiece,"
Vonnegut said in his 1969 address to the American Phys-

ical Society. "He sat down in an easy chair in the corner. He did not speak to anyone or change expression for half an hour. Then he got up, came back over to the mantelpiece, and picked up his cocktail glass, and he said to me, 'Nope.' "[18] *Ice-nine* apparently is impossible, but it is described by Vonnegut with the kind of scientific precision that Campbell himself would have admired.

Irving Langmuir's story may not be the only source of *ice-nine*, however. Vonnegut may have been influenced by Jules Verne, a writer whose tone, like Vonnegut's, is often flat, and who does not hesitate to stop to lecture his readers. One work by Verne, *Hector Servadac* (English title: *Off on a Comet*), is especially pertinent. A comet grazes the earth and carries a chunk of North Africa and the Mediterranean into space. As this small world whirls away from the sun, the temperature gets colder. The hero, Captain Servadac, and his assistant are on Gourbi Island, where the captain has a child throw a piece of ice into the sea, which in turn freezes solid. Verne explains that water under a condition of absolute stillness will remain liquid at several degrees below zero and that a slight shock will convert it to solid ice. This is not quite the same concept as *ice-nine*, but the catastrophic possibilities are much the same.

The point, of course, is not that Vonnegut read Jules Verne and was inspired by him (most likely he was not) but that Vonnegut, like other writers in the science-fiction vein, draws upon archetypes, stratagems, and contrivances that have by now been traded around so much within the form that they have become, in a way, common property. This is not to say, however, that they have lost their meaning. Vonnegut (though not to the same degree as John W. Campbell, Jr., and Hubbard) genuinely responds to the symbolic reality of many of the properties he relies upon. He believes in space travel, for instance, but for him it means a journey inward.

He has stated that he does not agree with Arthur C.

Clarke that the earth is our cradle and the solar system our kindergarten, and that it is our destiny to travel to the stars. Instead he prefers to cite Asimov's conception of three stages in human development: (1) Adventure dominant, (2) Technology dominant, and (3) Sociology dominant. Vonnegut's hope is that we are moving into stage three where we will turn our attention to "the cradle natures of Earthlings on Earth."[19]

Vonnegut also believes in the reality of time travel, but for him no time machine is necessary. In commenting on a book by Guy Murchie, *Music of the Spheres* (1961), he cites a concept from it that the few years each of us has are all the time there is, time that we go back and forth in. "I honestly believe," Vonnegut testifies, "I am tripping through time. Tomorrow I will be three years old again. The day after that I will be sixty-three."[20]

What Vonnegut is doing as he moves half mystically, half laughingly, in and out of science fiction is to try to come up with a definition of himself and others that will "stand in the terrifying light of twentieth-century knowledge."[21] When he is writing simply as a science-fiction writer in the stories he published in *Galaxy* ("Unready to Wear" and "The Big Trip Up Yonder") or in the *Magazine of Fantasy and Science Fiction* ("Harrison Bergeron"), he does not move very far toward that definition. But when he combines the special effects of science fiction with extended cosmic irony in his novels, he transforms one of the most important forms of pop culture into his own distinctive form of astral jokebook.

5

Adapting to Chaos

"*It is hard* to adapt to chaos," Vonnegut writes in *Breakfast of Champions*, "but it can be done. I am living proof of that: It can be done." In a major sense, Vonnegut's novels represent just such an adaptation. He moves steadily away from old-fashioned stories of the sort that lead readers to believe that life has leading characters and minor characters, important details and unimportant details, lessons to be learned in order to pass tests of physical, psychological, or spiritual strength, beginnings, middles, ends. By the time Vonnegut gets to *Breakfast of Champions*, he has resolved to avoid storytelling in favor of a kind of writing in which all persons are equally important and the only moral is to learn to adapt oneself to the requirements of chaos rather than to the requirements of an orderly universe (the most laughable and also the most fatal of illusions). Vonnegut accordingly chooses to utilize a fictional technique that relies upon radical juxtapositions of space-age gimmickry, schizophrenic religions, and a nonspatial time sense for purposes of social satire.

Such a technique is uniquely successful in *Slaughterhouse-Five*, and its development certainly places Vonnegut in the center of postwar avant gardism. But to many, Vonnegut remains more of a phenomenon than a writer to be taken seriously, his success more of an accidental product of the 1960s than anything else. But

101

even though there is some validity in this view, it is neither fair nor complete.

Vonnegut's popularity as a factor in his significance should be emphasized because it is one of the most important aspects of his achievement.

Vonnegut's approach, his manner, seems to spark a feeling of identification in many readers. This is more a matter of tone than it is a deliberate attempt to appeal to the "youth market." When one reads Vonnegut, explains John Skow in *Time* magazine, "it is as if a favorite uncle had just driven 1200 miles nonstop from Indianapolis, slugged down two stiff drinks, and collapsed on the sofa, body becalmed but mind still blasting along at 80 mph, voice spinning on and on, talking of horrors with rumpled brilliance."[1] Vonnegut comes across as a kindly relative, a decent fellow in a world of indecency, but suffering from it all just like the rest of us. "Vonnegut is an easy writer to feel affection for," Peter J. Reed writes in his study of Vonnegut. "Admittedly there are times when he seems a little coy or posed, but in general the personality behind the authorial voice is a pleasant one. From what he advocates and what he affirms, as well as from what he disapproves of, one senses a compassionate, gentle, troubled man."[2]

Vonnegut establishes what seems to be an essential and unusual bond between himself and his audience. Many writers have not at the same time been able to reach a mass audience and deal in an intellectual way with contemporary problems without an inevitable educational gap showing up. This alienation between writer and reader does not exist (or at least is not as extreme) in Vonnegut's case because he is able to make so many readers actually like him. He is the kindly uncle of American fiction, and this is a good thing for him to be. It is as if he is saying to his readers that, all right, he is cut off like them from the comforting myths of the past for which he longs and that all too often he lacks contact with others and feels isolated; but this does not mean that he cannot be kind.

Vonnegut's popularity can also be explained in terms of the attitudes he consistently expresses. Like so many of his readers in the 1960s, Vonnegut argues for the existence of multiple realities and multiple lifestyles, expresses a general disbelief in history and religion, tends to see himself as a victim of forces beyond his control, and despairs about any lasting hope for the human condition.[3] But through his willingness to suggest internalized solutions involving imagination and rationalizing fantasies, Vonnegut expresses what are essentially moral-uplift messages.

Nonetheless, Vonnegut masterfully uses his technique to present a view of self-destructive humanity working at full speed to destroy the world through global war, manic rates of reproduction, automation, pollution, political chauvinism, drugs, and good old greed. Vonnegut's planet is blasted by rampant technology and doomed by economic systems that are designed to drain it of its last drop of oil and extract from it the last shovelful of iron ore. And it does not look as if any of this will change until it is too late.

As pessimistic as this vision is, Vonnegut employs it for essentially comic purposes—and this is where the uplift comes in. He adopts the viewpoint of cosmic irony, which allows him to ridicule hilariously the comical absurdity of human attempts at alleviating chaos through self-contradicting philosophies and programs for living. At one point or another, Vonnegut parodies human faith in the efficacy of technology, in the soundness of capitalism, in the benefits of philanthropy, in the saving grace of religious systems, and in the social and intellectual values to be found in the traditional novel. His jibes are not always easy to take, and his manner often seems discouragingly stoical. But behind all of his novels is the voice of someone who is himself the victim of some too dimly apprehended, too late understood, cosmically ironic joke. And Vonnegut puts himself into several of his books as a character, just to make certain that he is seen taking his licks along with the rest of us.

Vonnegut's method does sometimes seem to go against his admittedly sentimental and even homely themes. Vonnegut does hold throughout to a pervasive and often dismaying skepticism or cool, but he does it with a mitigating earnestness that takes some of the hard edges off. He attacks the foolishness of Billy Pilgrim's mother and her misdirected religious fervor, and he makes fun of Malachi Constant's sense of purpose. But he simultaneously upholds the value of rationalizing fantasies in making life endurable, even though the cosmic response to any of them must be laughter. "In these edicts," Max Schulz writes, "he expresses an extreme and idealistic version of his midwestern middle-class values that nourished his Indiana boyhood. Similarly, his forthright, self-effacing, unadorned language is an implied rebuke of the double-speak that has assailed America from Joe McCarthy to Richard Nixon."[4]

Vonnegut does deserve to be taken seriously, both as a moralist and an artist. "His basic views," as Richard Bodtke points out, "are not profound or complex, but they are relevant, deeply felt, and (most important) transmuted into first-rate comic art."[5] He offers more than levity; he gives us an honest perception of the quality of twentieth-century life, and he creates a gnomic style that imposes a visionary end on his sense of discontinuity —even if it is summed up in his most famous aphorism, "So it goes."

Notes

1. REPORT ON THE VONNEGUT EFFECT

1. Kurt Vonnegut, Jr., *Wampeters, Foma, & Granfalloons* (New York: Delta, 1975), p. 282.
2. *Wampeters*, pp. 274–275.
3. *America Is West: An Anthology of Midwestern Life and Literature*, ed. John T. Flanagan (Minneapolis: University of Minnesota Press, 1945), p. iii.
4. Dan Wakefield, "In Vonnegut's Karass," in *The Vonnegut Statement*, ed. Jerome Klinkowitz and John Somer (New York: Delta, 1973), p. 63.
5. Richard Todd, "*Breakfast of Champions:* This Novel Contains More than Twice Your Minimum Daily Requirement of Irony," *Atlantic* (May 1973), p. 108.
6. I am indebted for this term to Wayne L. James, *The Fractured Vision: A Study of the Novels of Kurt Vonnegut, Jr.*, M.A. Thesis, St. Cloud State University, 1974.
7. *Wampeters*, p. 163.
8. *Wampeters*, p. 240.
9. *Wampeters*, pp. 254–255.
10. *Wampeters*, p. 285.
11. *Wampeters*, p. 259.
12. For most of the information on Vonnegut's college writing, I am indebted to Robert Scholes, "Chasing a Lone Eagle: Vonnegut's College Writing," in *The Vonnegut Statement*, pp. 45–54.
13. Scholes, p. 47.
14. R. A. Sokolov, *Newsweek*, 19 Aug. 1968, p. 85.

15. Richard Rhodes, *Book World*, 18 Aug. 1968, p. 4.
16. Terry Southern, *New York Times Book Review*, 2 June 1963, p. 20.
17. Leslie Fiedler, "The Divine Stupidity of Kurt Vonnegut," *Esquire*, Sept. 1970, p. 196.
18. *Wampeters*, p. 235.
19. Raymond M. Olderman, *Beyond the Waste Land: The American Novel in the Nineteen-Sixties* (New Haven: Yale University Press, 1972), p. 191.
20. Joe David Bellamy, "Kurt Vonnegut for President: The Making of an Academic Reputation," in *The Vonnegut Statement*, p. 81.
21. *Wampeters*, p. 100.
22. *Wampeters*, p. 276.
23. *Wampeters*, p. xxv.
24. *Wampeters*, p. xxv.
25. *Wampeters*, p. 56.
26. *Wampeters*, p. 157.
27. *Wampeters*, p. 237.
28. *Wampeters*, pp. 228–229.
29. *Wampeters*, p. 165.
30. *Wampeters*, p. 92.
31. Olderman, p. 192.

2. COSMIC IRONY

1. Unless otherwise indicated, I am indebted for much of the following information on black humor to Max F. Schulz, "Black Humor," *Encyclopedia of World Literature in the 20th Century* (New York: Frederick Ungar, 1975), IV, 45–49.
2. Robert Scholes, "A Talk with Kurt Vonnegut, Jr.," in *The Vonnegut Statement*, ed. Jerome Klinkowitz and John Somer (New York: Delta, 1973), p. 96.
3. Gerald Weales, "What Ever Happened to Tugboat Annie?" *The Reporter*, 1 Dec. 1966, p. 50.
4. Raymond M. Olderman, *Beyond the Waste Land: The American Novel in the Nineteen-Sixties* (New Haven: Yale University Press, 1972), pp. 26–27.

5. Kurt Vonnegut, Jr., *Wampeters, Foma, & Granfalloons* (New York: Delta, 1975), p. 258.
6. Vance Bourjaily, "What Vonnegut Is and Isn't," *New York Times Book Review*, 13 Aug. 1972, p. 3.
7. Leonard Leff, "Utopia Reconstructed: Alienation in Vonnegut's *God Bless You, Mr. Rosewater*," *Critique*, No. 3, 1971, pp. 29–30.
8. Peter J. Reed, *Kurt Vonnegut, Jr.* (New York: Warner, 1972), p. 208.
9. For a good comparison of Vonnegut and Lewis in terms of *Player Piano*, see Mary Sue Shriber, "You've Come a Long Way, Babbitt! From Zenith to Ilium," *Twentieth Century Literature*, April 1971, pp. 101–106.
10. Charles Lee, *Saturday Review of Literature*, 30 Aug. 1952, p. 17.
11. Granville Hicks, *New York Times Book Review*, 17 Aug. 1952, p. 5.
12. Robert Scholes, *The Fabulators* (New York: Oxford University Press, 1967), p. 45.
13. Tim Hildebrand, "Two or Three Things I Know About Kurt Vonnegut's Imagination," in *The Vonnegut Statement*, p. 122.
14. Charles B. Harris, *Contemporary American Novelists of the Absurd* (New Haven: College and University Press, 1971), pp. 54–60.
15. Jerome Klinkowitz, "Kurt Vonnegut, Jr., and the Crime of His Times," *Critique*, No. 3 1971, pp. 38–53.
16. Richard Schickel, *Harpers*, May 1966, p. 103.
17. John R. May, *Toward a New Earth: Apocalypse in the American Novel* (Notre Dame, Ind.: University of Notre Dame Press, 1972), p. 199.
18. Reed, p. 152.
19. Daniel Talbot, *Book Week*, 11 April 1965, p. 6.
20. For more information on the Dresden Raid, see David Irving, *The Destruction of Dresden* (New York: Ballantine Books, 1963). For another literary treatment, see the drama *Soldiers: An Obituary for Geneva* (1968) by the West German playwright Rolf Hochhuth.
21. Jerome Klinkowitz, "Kurt Vonnegut, Jr.: The Canary in a Cathouse," in *The Vonnegut Statement*, p. 16.

22. *Wampeters*, p. 184.
23. Robert Scholes, *New York Times Book Review*, 6 April 1969, p. 1.
24. *Wampeters*, p. 251.
25. *Wampeters*, p. 252.
26. *Wampeters*, p. 281.
27. John Barth, "The Literature of Exhaustion," cited by Hassan Ihab, *Contemporary American Literature*, 1945–1972 (New York: Frederick Ungar, 1973), p. 56.
28. Stanley Schatt, "The World of Kurt Vonnegut, Jr.," *Critique*, No. 3 1971, p. 67.

3. THE "NEW REALITY" OF *SLAUGHTERHOUSE-FIVE*

1. Cited by Alfred Kazin, *Bright Book of Life: American Novelists and Storytellers from Hemingway to Mailer* (Boston: Atlantic/Little, Brown, 1973), p. 81.
2. P. S. Prescott, *Newsweek*, 14 May 1973, p. 114.
3. Robert Scholes, *New York Times Book Review*, 6 April 1969, p. 1.
4. Kurt Vonnegut, Jr., *Wampeters, Foma & Granfalloons* (New York: Delta, 1975), p. 280.
5. Jerry H. Bryant. *The Open Decision* (New York: Free Press, 1970), p. 36.
6. Bryant, p. 22.
7. Bertrand Russell, *The ABC of Relativity* (London: Kegan Paul, 1925), p. 209.
8. Charles B. Harris, *Contemporary American Novelists of the Absurd* (New Haven: College and University Press, 1971), p. 74.
9. For a detailed study of the Wells-James debate, see Leon Edel and Gordon N. Ray, *Henry James and H. G. Wells* (Urbana: University of Illinois Press, 1958).
10. Karen and Charles Wood, "The Vonnegut Effect: Science Fiction and Beyond," in *The Vonnegut Statement*, p. 154.
11. *Time*, 10 April 1972, p. 77.
12. Tim Hildebrand, "Two or Three Things I Know about Kurt Vonnegut's Imagination," in *The Vonnegut Statement*, p. 132.

4. SCIENCE FICTION

1. Kurt Vonnegut, Jr., *Wampeters, Foma, & Granfalloons* (New York: Delta, 1975), p. 1.

2. Brian W. Aldiss, *Billion Year Spree: The True History of Science Fiction* (New York: Doubleday, 1973), pp. 314, 316.

3. Leslie Fiedler, "The Divine Stupidity of Kurt Vonnegut," *Esquire*, Sept. 1970, p. 198.

4. G. K. Wolfe, "Vonnegut and the Metaphor of Science Fiction: *The Sirens of Titan*," *Journal of Popular Culture*, Spring 1972, p. 969.

5. Vonnegut, *Wampeters*, p. 262.

6. *Modern Science Fiction*, ed. Norman Spinrad (New York: Anchor), pp. 4–5. I am indebted to Spinrad for much of the following information on the development of science fiction.

7. Vonnegut, *Wampeters*, p. 261.

8. *Modern Science Fiction*, p. 11.

9. *Modern Science Fiction*, p. 13.

10. Aldiss, p. 314.

11. "A Sci-Fi Faith," *Time*, 22 March 1976, p. 57.

12. *Modern Science Fiction*, p. 110.

13. Aldiss, p. 257.

14. *Modern Science Fiction*, p. 271.

15. Karen and Charles Wood, "The Vonnegut Effect: Science Fiction and Beyond," in *The Vonnegut Statement*, ed. Jerome Klinkowitz and John Somer (New York: Delta, 1973), pp. 144–146.

16. Aldiss, p. 314.

17. "Kilgore Trout," *Venus on the Half-Shell* (New York: Dell, 1975), p. 204.

18. Vonnegut, *Wampeters*, p. 97.

19. Vonnegut, *Wampeters*, p. 83.

20. Vonnegut, *Wampeters*, p. xxvi.

21. Aldiss, p. 253.

5.   ADAPTING TO CHAOS

1. John Skow, *Time*, 3 June 1974, p. 77.
2. Peter J. Reed, *Kurt Vonnegut, Jr.* (New York: Warner, 1972), p. 219.
3. Richard Todd, *"Breakfast of Champions:* This Novel Contains More than Twice Your Minimum Daily Requirement of Irony," *Atlantic*, May 1973, p. 108.
4. Richard Bodtke, "Great Sorrows, Small Joys: The World of Kurt Vonnegut, Jr.," *Cross Currents*, Winter 1970, p. 120.

Bibliography

1. WORKS BY KURT VONNEGUT

NOVELS
Player Piano. New York: Charles Scribner's Sons, 1952.
The Sirens of Titan. New York: Dell, 1959.
Mother Night. New York: Fawcett, 1962.
Cat's Cradle. New York: Holt, Rinehart and Winston, 1963.
God Bless You, Mr. Rosewater. New York: Holt, Rinehart and Winston, 1965.
Slaughterhouse-Five. New York: Delacorte/Seymour Lawrence, 1969.
Breakfast of Champions. New York: Delacorte/Seymour Lawrence, 1973.
Slapstick. New York: Delacorte/Seymour Lawrence, 1976.

STORIES AND SHORT WORKS
Canary in a Cat House. New York: Fawcett, 1961.
Welcome to the Monkey House. New York: Delacorte/Seymour Lawrence, 1968.
Wampeters, Foma, & Granfalloons. New York: Delacorte/Seymour Lawrence, 1974.

PLAYS
Happy Birthday, Wanda June. New York: Delacorte/Seymour Lawrence, 1971.
Between Time and Timbuktu, or Prometheus—5. New York: Delacorte/Seymour Lawrence, 1972.

2. WORKS ABOUT KURT VONNEGUT

BIBLIOGRAPHIES
Hudgens, Betty L. *Kurt Vonnegut, Jr.: A Checklist.* Detroit:
  Gale Research Co., 1972.
Pieratt, Asa B., Jr. and Klinkowitz, Jerome. *Kurt Vonnegut,
  Jr.: A Descriptive Bibliography and Annotated Sec-
  ondary Checklist.* Archon Books (The Shoe String Press,
  Inc.), 1974.

SPECIAL ISSUES OF JOURNALS
"Vonnegut." *Critique*, 12 (Number 3, 1971).
"Kurt Vonnegut, Jr.: A Symposium." *Summary*, 1 (Number
  2, 1971).

ESSAYS AND BOOKS
Aldiss, Brian W. *Billion Year Spree: The True History of
  Science Fiction.* New York: Doubleday, 1973, pp. 313–
  316.
Bodtke, Richard. "Great Sorrows, Small Joys: The World of
  Kurt Vonnegut, Jr." *Cross Currents*, 20 (Winter 1970),
  120.
Bourjaily, Vance. "What Vonnegut Is and Isn't." *New York
  Times Book Review* (13 August 1972), pp. 3, 10.
Bryan, C.D.B. "Vonnegut on Target." *The New Republic*
  (8 October 1966), pp. 21–26.
Bryant, Jerry H. *The Open Decision.* New York: Free Press,
  1970, pp. 303–324.
De Mott, Benjamin. "Vonnegut's Otherworldly Laughter."
  Saturday Review, 54 (1 May 1971), 29–32, 38.
Engel, David. "On the Question of Foma: A Study of the
  Novels of Kurt Vonnegut, Jr." *Riverside Quarterly*, 5
  (February 1972), 119–128.
Fiedler, Leslie. "The Divine Stupidity of Kurt Vonnegut."
  Esquire, 74 (September 1970), 195–97, 199–200, 202–
  204.
Goldsmith, David. *Kurt Vonnegut: Fantasist of Fire and Ice.*
  Popular Writers Series. Bowling Green: Bowling Green
  University Popular Press, 1972.

Harris, Charles B. *Contemporary American Novelists of the Absurd.* New Haven: College and University Press, 1971, pp. 51–75.

Hauck, Richard Boyd. *A Cheerful Nihilism.* Bloomington: Indiana University Press, 1971, pp. 237–245.

Hendin, Josephine. "Writer as Culture Hero." *Harpers* (July 1974), pp. 82–87.

Ihab, Hassan. *Contemporary American Literature, 1945–1972.* New York: Frederick Ungar, 1973, pp. 45–47, 65, 86.

Kael, Pauline. "Current Cinema." *New Yorker*, 46 (23 January 1971), 76–78.

Kazin, Alfred. *Bright Book of Life: American Novelists and Storytellers from Hemingway to Mailer.* Boston: Atlantic/Little Brown, 1973, pp. 82–83, 86–90.

Kennedy, R. C. "Kurt Vonnegut, Jr." *Art International*, 15 (May 1971), 20–25.

Leverence, W. John. "*Cat's Cradle* and Traditional American Humor." *Journal of Popular Culture*, 4 (Spring 1972), 955–963.

May, John R. *Toward a New Earth: Apocalypse in the American Novel.* Notre Dame, Indiana: University of Notre Dame Press, 1972, pp. 172–200.

McCabe, Loretta. "An Exclusive Interview with Kurt Vonnegut, Jr." *Writer's Yearbook—1970*, pp. 92–95, 100–101, 103–105.

McNelly, Willis E. "Science Fiction—The Modern Mythology," in *Science Fiction: The Other Side of Realism*, ed. Thomas D. Clareson. Bowling Green: Bowling Green University Popular Press, 1971, pp. 193–198.

Olderman, Raymond M. *Beyond the Waste Land: The American Novel in the Nineteen-Sixties.* New Haven: Yale University Press, 1972, pp. 189–219.

Pauly, Rebecca M. "The Moral Stance of Kurt Vonnegut," *Extrapolation*, 15 (December 1973), 66–71.

Ranley, Ernest W. "What Are People For?" *Commonweal*, 94 (7 May 1971), 207–211.

Reed, Peter J. *Kurt Vonnegut, Jr.* New York: Warner, 1972.

Rovit, Earl. "Some Shapes in Recent American Fiction." *Contemporary Literature* (Autumn 1974), pp. 550–565.

Samuels, Charles Thomas. "Age of Vonnegut." *New Repub-lic*, 164 (12 June 1971), 30–32.

Scholes, Robert. *The Fabulators*. New York: Oxford University Press, 1967, pp. 35–55.

Schriber, Mary Sue. "You've Come a Long Way, Babbitt! From Zenith to Ilium." *Twentieth Century Literature*, 17 (April 1971), 101–106.

Schulz, Max F. "Black Humor." *Encyclopedia of World Literature in the 20th Century*. New York: Frederick Ungar, IV. 45–49.

———. *Black Humor Fiction of the Sixties*. Athens: Ohio University Press, 1973, pp. 32–65.

Tanner, Tony. *City of Words*. New York: Harper and Row, 1971, pp. 181–201.

The Vonnegut Statement. Ed. Jerome Klinkowitz and John Somer. New York: Delta, 1973.

Weales, Gerald. "What Ever Happened to Tugboat Annie?" *The Reporter*, 35 (1 December 1966), 50, 52–56.

Wolfe, G. K. "Vonnegut and the Metaphor of Science Fiction: *The Sirens of Titan*." *Journal of Popular Culture*, 4 (Spring 1972), 964–969.

Wood, Michael. "Dancing in the Dark." *New York Review of Books*, 20 (31 May 1973), 23–25.

Index

MODERN LITERATURE MONOGRAPHS

In the same series (continued from page ii)